AUSTRALIA

AUSTRALIA
· Beyond the Dreamtime ·

THOMAS KENEALLY
PATSY ADAM-SMITH
ROBYN DAVIDSON

Facts On File

New York • Oxford

Opposite: An early comic strip depicting the changing fortunes in the relations between Europeans and Aborigines. 'White fella soon kill all black fella,' said one tribesman in 1830

Australia: Beyond the Dreamtime
Here Nature Is Reversed: © Thomas Keneally 1987
The Road from Gundagai: © Patsy Adam-Smith 1987
The Mythological Crucible: © Robyn Davidson 1987

Published by arrangement with BBC Books
a division of BBC Enterprises Ltd.

Facts On File, Inc.
460 Park Avenue South
New York, New York 10016

Library of Congress Catalog Number: 88-046176

ISBN 0-8160-1922-3

The publishers would like to thank the following for giving permission to quote from published material in copyright:

Cambell Connelly, extracts from *The Road to Gundagai* by Jack O'Hagan; Angus and Robertson, Australia for *Nationality* and *No Foe Shall Gather Our Harvest* plus extracts by Mary Gilmore. (In spite of all efforts we have been unable to trace the publishers of Helen Power.)

Facts On File books are available at special discounts when purchased in bulk quantities for businesses, associations, institutions, or sales promotion. Please contact the Special Sales Department at 212/683-2244.
(Dial 1-800-322-8755, except in NY, AK, HI)

Printed in the United States of America

10 9 8 7 6 5 4 3 2 1

This book is printed on acid-free paper.

INDIAN OCEAN

TIMOR SEA

Darwin

Arnhem Land

NORTHERN

TERRITORY

Broome

Great Sandy Desert

Macdonnell Range

Alice Springs

Hamersley Range

Gibson Desert

Musgrave Ranges

WESTERN AUSTRALIA

Great Victoria Desert

SOUTH

Nullarbor Plain

Kalgoorlie

Perth
Fremantle

Swan
River

Canning River

Great Australian Bight

Port Augusta

SOUTH AUSTRALIAN BASIN

0   500 Miles

0   800 Km

Contents

PART 2 The Road from Gundagai

PART 3 The Mythological Crucible

PART 1 Here Nature is Reversed

THOMAS KENEALLY

Many people, including D. H. Lawrence and Patrick White, have commented on the grand indifference to European sensitivity which the Australian landscape emits. A character in Lawrence's *Kangaroo,* set in the 1920s, says – looking out of a train on the coastal mountains of New South Wales – 'It looks as if no man had ever loved it.' Lawrence was simply echoing such cries as those of Major Robbie Ross of the first convict fleet: 'Here nature is reversed.'

Australia still exudes this unwillingness to come to terms with what Europeans expect the earth to be. It was very hard for the ice-blue God of northern Europe to take on credibility in the Australian landscape, and those who came early – to administer, to serve time or to settle – felt that there were other gods and other values inherent in the place. For most of the two hundred years of European settlement of Australia, newcomers have been torn between a sense of alienation and a frantic curiosity, and these two reactions were reflected in the work of Australian artists and writers until well into the twentieth century.

What Europeans first saw as the alien quality of Australia made them presume that the continent was *terra nullius* – vacant space. 'Do you have a map?' asks a sponsor of the expedition of the German explorer Voss in Patrick White's novel of that name. 'The map?' answers Voss. 'I shall first make it.' This response was pretty representative of European ideas about Australia. It was void, and they would mark and somehow redeem it.

But there was a map, in fact a series of maps, of Australia, and Australia was no vacant lot. When and if the Ming Dynasty sailors, operating from Ambon

in the Celebes, landed briefly near Darwin, this map of the hinterland had already long existed. Similarly, when the sixteenth-century Portuguese traced the coast of northern Australia, and the seventeenth-century Dutch visited the western coast and expressed a lack of desire for it as real estate, the map existed. And, of course, when James Cook, the nonpareil navigator, found his way to the eastern coast in 1770, the map had been in existence for millennia – one could say for aeons. To the people who had made the map Australia was not alien or puzzling or a denial of Europe, but absolutely central and self-explanatory.

If Australian Aboriginal peoples got a mention at all in the classrooms where my generation had their schooling, we were told that they had come to the Australian continent in three waves across land bridges from the direction of Indonesia, some thirty thousand years past. The latest archaeology – based mainly on the examination of camp sites – indicates that that period of Aboriginal occupation could have begun as much as one hundred thousand years ago. This is an astounding time line and would have yielded half a million generations of tribal people. An acknowledgment of them – of the fact that they had a remarkable sense of title to their tribal earth, and that they never surrendered that title to the Europeans through any treaty or covenant – has justly to introduce any story of the European settlement of Australia.

Long before the death of Caesar or the birth of Christ, therefore, there were some six hundred tribes and six hundred separate languages on the Australian mainland and in what the Europeans originally called Van Diemen's Land and is now called Tasmania. There were, just to give a few examples, the Iwaija people of Arnhem Land; the Walpiri, Aranda, Pitjatjantjara and Pintobi of central Australia; and the Eora people, a relationship of four separate tribes who occupied the choice and temperate area of what would later become Sydney. The word *eora*, in the Sydney language, simply meant humankind.

According to the Aboriginals these tribal areas had been created out of void earth by hero ancestors in a period known as the Dreamtime. Trails which criss-cross the tribal earth from one waterhole to another, from one food source to another, had also been created by the hero ancestors, and the Aboriginal followed them in daily life, maintaining them and enriching them through ceremonial and magic. One tribe might share hero ancestors with another, so that the Dreaming trails might run across a number of tribal boundaries. In areas rich in rainfall, sources of food and vegetation, these trails might run for less than sixty miles. But in the great deserts of the centre, where clan groups were more widely scattered and where people had to walk further to collect the bounty of the earth – euro, wallaby, kangaroo-rat, nardoo, yam – the trails could run for a thousand miles or more.

Aboriginal culture by its nature was concerned with conserving the earth in the strictest sense, though as the Australian historian Geoffrey Blainey argues, that did not mean that Aboriginals did not transform the face of Australia.

Opposite: Though Australia has been settled by Europeans for two hundred years, Aboriginals have inhabited the continent for perhaps a hundred thousand years

They brought with them their native dogs, for example, which are credited with killing out a number of mainland species including one fetchingly named the great marsupial wombat. And they cleared the earth by using fire to drive animals out of hiding. But everything they did in their daily lives was concerned with a repetition of the behaviour of their ancestors, and on a concept of the earth as both eternal yet dependent for its maintenance on the fulfilment of certain rites.

Their picture of the earth was therefore bound to suffer a frightful shock at their first contact with Europeans. It was to be a shock even more radical than that which would be experienced by the Maoris of New Zealand, who had occupied their benign South Seas islands only since about the eighth century AD and who in any case had a concept of land ownership more akin to that harboured by Europeans. The anthropologist Aldo Marsola says that, about the time of the first European contact with Aboriginals on the east coast of Australia, a rumour ran through the tribes of the south-east of the continent that one of the pillars that held the sky up had slipped, and that stars and spirits were falling to earth over towards the east.

Inevitably comparisons are always made between the settlement of Australia and that of other new countries, such as America or Canada. But there is one vast and fundamental difference between Australia and the rest. The north-eastern seaboard of the USA, for example, was voluntarily settled by righteous Puritan brethren. There were later many poor indentured labourers and convicts, and of course the African slaves in their chains. But it is true of Americans as a race that they see themselves as spiritual if not actual descendants of the Pilgrims, and they celebrate the Thanksgiving of the godly Pilgrims every year. Australia, on the other hand, was settled involuntarily by those who were – by decree of the British courts – unjust and unlikely to experience any redemption.

James Cook's report of his location of a vast coastline in 1770, and in particular his sojourn in a particular inlet – Botany Bay, a shallow anchorage south of the present site of Sydney – was greeted in Europe with the same avidity as we would show for information brought back from Jupiter. Scientists were particularly stimulated by the reports of Cook and the chief of his scientific team, Sir Joseph Banks. But so also were social theorists. Sir Joseph Banks himself promoted Botany Bay to a House of Commons committee in 1779 as a suitable penal station. Being in such a deep pocket of the universe, it would be likely to retain anyone sent there even for a brief sentence; and being spacious, new and marvellous, it might also be capable of rehabilitating the criminal.

The reasons for initiating the system of transportation of felons to Australia have been written about a great deal – badly in the textbooks whose pages we turned in the humid classrooms of our Australian childhood summers; well by a number of recent Australian writers, notably Robert Hughes in *The Fatal*

Shore. Much has been written, too, about how the new machines were displacing traditional British crafts and the new agriculture driving people off the land. As a schoolchild in Australia I studied Goldsmith's 'The Deserted Village', though it was not pointed out to me that some of the people from 'The Deserted Village' were probably in Phillip's convict transports.

Amidst the social dislocation in England people drifted to the cities; here child prostitution and addiction to Holland waters – recorded by Hogarth – were common; most cities had their Gin Lanes. Minor and often vicious crime was endemic. What the machine and Gin Lane were doing to Georgian civilisation, the microchip and Smack Alley are doing to the developed world, including modern Australia. There are great parallels between the modern age and the Georgian.

The Georgians reacted to the social crisis by strenuous legislation. There were over sixty crimes punishable by death. They were mostly crimes against property, and included various degrees of poaching and the stealing of lead from church roofs. Juries were often – according to their lights – merciful in valuing stolen property; for otherwise the gallows would never have been vacant, especially in a society so unshocked by hangings that even a refined soul like James Boswell might drag his friend Sir Joshua Reynolds down to Newgate Arch to see the hangings.

In the plague of crime which at present afflicts most developed countries, the late Georgian era seems to be a history lesson that simple-minded application of stiff sentences is on its own not enough. Yet it is a little amazing and maybe a little significant that even in modern Australian society, when crime and punishment are discussed, the Georgian genesis of Australia is rarely referred to. Even in that savage age, when petty crime could attract a seven-year sentence, many of those condemned to death had their sentences commuted from death to transportation for fourteen or seven years. But there was nowhere to transport them any more. The gaols of Britain were, as our childhood history books liked to say, 'crammed with convicts', many of them young; and conditions behind bars attracted the attention of the leading reformers of the day.

Excess convicts were placed on disused naval vessels – hulks – throughout the harbours and estuaries of Britain. Each hulk was a little offshore penal settlement, but none of them was far enough offshore to suit the Home Secretary. The loss in 1776 of the American colonies, which had once taken convicts ashore as indentured labourers, ensured that the proposal of Botany Bay as an ideal prison periodically resurfaced.

The official sentences of some of the criminals sent to Australia, especially in the First Fleet, show how thinking about possible remote penal stations altered throughout the 1780s. In 1782 sentences, Nova Scotia was still mentioned as a possible destination. In 1784, the sentences name Africa. John Moorin, for example, tried before Mr Recorder at the Old Bailey for stealing two silver

tablespoons, value ten shillings, was ordered to be transported to Africa, as were most of the other convicts sentenced in the same sessions. Moorin's destination would ultimately be even more remote than the one to which Mr Recorder consigned him.

It used to be argued that the cause of transportation to New South Wales was entirely a matter of overcrowding of the gaols and the legal system. Geoffrey Blainey created a stir in the 1960s by arguing that the British principally wanted to exploit the tall spires of the Norfolk pines and the native flax plants which Captain Cook had seen on Norfolk Island, far out in the Pacific, and that the convict settlement at Botany Bay was intended to serve merely as a base from which to reach these valuable resources. To the British, Norfolk Island would have been the Georgian equivalent of the modern discovery of oil in, say, the Hebrides. It could have made eighteenth-century Britain independent of risky supplies from the Baltic and given it a new freedom of action. Others have argued that the British wanted a secure port on the route via the Southern Ocean between Europe and the tea supplies of Canton. But whatever historians say about the causes of Australia's foundation, its nature has marked Australian society and popular culture ever since.

Opposite above: The notorious penal settlement at Macquarie Harbour in Van Diemen's Land (Tasmania), sketched by a convict artist, William Buelow Gould

Those who want to experience Sydney Cove with the same eyes as the first British arrivals can take the Manly–Sydney ferry. You travel in a deep channel, gouged by a glacier, down a magnificent harbour in one of whose coves the city of Sydney stands. Once in Sydney Cove, you know within feet or inches where the first European things happened. In the political, civil and judicial sense, for example, Australia began with the reading of a proclamation by what is now a bus stop in Loftus Street.

Opposite below: Convicts at Sydney Gaol, 'their crimes written on their foreheads and in their eyes'. Many were transported for offences that would seem trifling today

The first time I made this wonderful small journey from Manly to Sydney – at least the first time that I remember – was as a child down from the bush in 1942. The Japanese were at that stage revealing our Asian location to us by bombing some of our more tropical ports like Darwin and Broome, and the *Queen Mary* – loaded with troops newly returned from their rather remote imperial duty in the Middle East – was poking its way through the Harbour's august heads. But in that historic crisis, of which even I was aware, I still don't think I could look at the harbour without thinking almost instantly of the much earlier, bizarre origins of the Australian nation. For one thing, Australian mothers always pointed out to their children the fortified small island named Pinchgut, which from the start served as a place of extra punishment for anonymous ancestors called convicts.

Into this great space of harbour there drifted in late January 1788 a most remarkable flotilla of small ships. They had sailed fifteen thousand miles to the nether side of the universe. In Georgian terms they had penetrated deep space, and most of them were now committed to living in it for good. The harbour had been first seen by a European only a day or two before – by the commander of that first penal fleet. In the spirit of later emigration to Australia, Phillip's professed allegiance was British, but his genes were mixed – his father was a Frankfurt language and dance instructor and may have been Jewish. Phillip himself was a middle-aged farmer and half-pay naval officer from Hampshire who had been given the task of establishing European society of a very eccentric and particular nature on this remote planet.

The coastline on which the harbour stood (it was still just a harbour, and not – as it would later become – *the* Harbour) was known as New South Wales. The inlet stood seven miles north of Botany Bay, the place which Cook had made the most famous distant star in the European world-picture, and for which various planners saw various possibilities – as a home for those Americans loyal to George III, or as a prison, the most distant and most expansive gulag in history. Arthur Phillip's fleet had, however, found Botany Bay shallow, unsuitable for major settlement and vulnerable to the east wind. Reconnoitring north, he found a gap which Cook had named perfunctorily Port Jackson, and – beyond its heads – this wonder of a harbour which until then had been known only to the Eora tribespeople of the region.

The Eora were not about to encounter normal European society, for in the holds of Arthur Phillip's ships sat some seven hundred and fifty convicted British felons. They had travelled eight months to get here. They had not been allowed ashore in any port. Many of them had been aboard ship, chained and unchained, for more than a year. Each on his or her eighteen inches of bedspace, the convict looked out through the portholes of the convict transport at the fine but highly individual reaches of Sydney Harbour and at a weird new world.

There is a fascination inherent in the question of who these people were, these Australian first-comers, these fallen Adams and Eves, their crimes written on their foreheads and in their eyes and emphasised by their chains. The question of the identity of the guards and administrators pales a little by comparison. I cannot claim any kinship with the first fleet (though I had a Fenian forbear in the very last convict ship, the *Hougoumont*, eighty years later). But it seems that every Australian does understand, with either fear or fascination, that part of what he is, part of his vision of the world is based on who these people were, and what their government thought of them, and why they were sent so far.

If you had, for example, been aboard the transport *Lady Penrhyn* on the day it tacked in through Sydney heads you might have known an Australian Eve called Mary Brenham, a girl of humble enough crimes and fallibilities and ambitions. In November 1784 Mary had stolen two stuffed petticoats, a pair of stays, four and a half yards of cloth, a waistcoat, a cap, a pair of cotton stockings, etc., etc., the property of her London employer, Mr John Kennedy. She had been sentenced to seven years' transportation to Africa, since Africa was in 1784 the supposed destination the government would choose for English convicts. A minister of religion made a clemency plea to the court on her mother's

behalf. The court records say under the heading of age: 'The prisoner is not yet
fourteen years.' When her transport entered Sydney, and its passengers saw the
same deep olive shores you still see from the Manly ferry, she was carrying at
her breast the illegitimate son a sailor had begot on her. She would never leave
the place.

The name 'Australia' – derived from *Australis*, the Latin word for south –
had not yet been devised for this continent; in fact it was not even known
whether the New South Wales of Captain Cook connected up with the western
New Holland of the Dutch. Phillip was none the less unabashed about claiming,
hard by what is now that bus stop in Loftus Street, the immense and unknown
hinterland for that distant George III who had so recently lost another hinterland
in the Americas. He specifically chose a deep anchorage cove, which today has
the Opera House on one side, the ugly Cahill Expressway backing it and the
fascinating area called the Rocks on the western arm. He named the place
Sydney Cove, and that was appropriate, since Lord Sydney, the Home Secretary
of the government of Pitt the Younger, was a robust political hack of the type
who would later proliferate in Australian politics. Eleven ships were to drop
anchor around this deep cove and land their supplies and their fallen people.
The flagship was named *Sirius* after the dog star, a suitable constellation to look
over the dog days of an Australian January, deep summer in that part of the
world.

The cross-harbour ferry on which you will take your Manly-to-Sydney trip
is more than twice the tonnage of the largest of those ships which brought the
first European Australians. We can call them Australians – irrespective of
quibbles over dates – as early as this, I think, because they had been renounced
by the known world. The idea was that New South Wales was so distant that
no one could return from it except by government arrangement or some
miracle of sudden wealth. For Mary Brenham and her companions, as for most
of the others who were to follow in convict ships for another eighty years, the
government and the deity would avoid making such arrangements.

The penal transportation system was the institution which had made Australia
attractive to Europeans then. And it was criticised from the start by both liberals
and conservatives. One critic said that the convicts could have been dealt with
at less expense if clothed in velvet and sustained on claret and venison at
restaurants in the Strand. If there is truth in Blainey's Norfolk Island pine-and-
flax theory, the government was soon disappointed. The Norfolk pines were
knotty and the flax did not flourish.

It has to be said that, even though penal, the First Fleet established standards
of health and stability for its day. Only thirty-five people died on the enormous
voyage. You would have been hard put to find in Britain a village of some
fifteen hundred people in which so few deaths occurred over a year. This
statistic raises a question on which I and most other Australians cannot make
up our minds. Were those Georgian gentlemen who controlled the First Fleet

Opposite below: Botany Bay Aborigines demonstrating their skill at climbing trees while hunting
Below: The arrival of the Europeans, who introduced the Aborigines to alcohol, inevitably debased the noble savage

Above: 'Even the
animals seemed to
assert this otherness.'
The nocturnal platy-
pus, a furry, duck-
billed, web-footed, egg-
laying mammal, epito-
mises Australia's
unique animal life

21

refined and educated barbarians on the lines of Hitler's *Einsatzgruppen*, or were they cultivated people, or were they both? Given the place that the convict occupies in Australian myth, we were always of course quite willing to believe the worst of them, and over the penal period in Australia both the most remarkable of visionaries and the most pitiable sadists would find a place for themselves. And there is something else: amongst both the officers and the prisoners there were those who landed with dread and who looked on the strange shore with horror. And there were those who looked upon it with avidity, either because of its scientific curiosity or because of its human possibility. Such was to be the pattern of European attitudes to Australia for the next two hundred years. The rule Australia imposed on everyone from the start was that you had to take it on its own terms, and they were very individual terms.

The ship's chandlers of Portsmouth, Plymouth and the Thames had used the amazing lengths to which the fleet was to travel as an excuse for unloading on to it all their indifferent and mouldy wares. It was clear to any thinking member of the fleet that food had to be quickly raised from this new earth so indifferent to their needs. Phillip discovered, though, that his criminals were victims of the great reforms in industry and agriculture, and were neither industrious nor agricultural. Too many of them were confidence tricksters and pickpockets and whores, more used to working the crowd in front of the Royal Theatre in Covent Garden than to clearing the new earth.

But again the problem was not simply the inexpertness of the lags. It was the very wrong-headedness of the new world. The hardwoods were so hard that they split axes. The seasons were inverted. European seed, planted in the earth, withered. The trees shed leaves either not at all or continuously. The trouble was that the gods who dominated the European landscape were totally absent here. There was a sense of other gods, gods ancient, Aboriginal, and therefore shocking to the European soul.

Even the animals seemed to assert this otherness. They were absurd and from before the Ark. This glorious and perverse absurdity can be seen in the platypus house at Sydney's Taronga Park Zoo, which is kept perpetually dark to deceive the platypus into pursuing its nocturnal habits. The animal is duck-billed, has fur and webbed feet, lays eggs and yet suckles its young. This is what the garrison commander, Major Ross, meant when he made his complaint about nature being reversed in this place.

If in the settlement which would grow to become European Australia there was wide disapproval of this sort of new world, there was perhaps an even greater disapproval of the Aboriginal peoples. Sydney Aboriginals called the new arrivals, with more wisdom than they knew, *turuga* – fallen stars. Within a year of the Sydney landing a virulent epidemic of smallpox ate through the Eora people, who had never seen such a thing before. To them it must have had the horror and impact that a virus introduced from Venus or Jupiter would hold for us. Some Aboriginal males were captured for the purposes of turning them into ambassadors between the lags and the tribespeople. The first such ambassador, kidnapped on the beach at Manly, was a young man called Arabanoo. Before dying of smallpox in the Governor's residence, Arabanoo cast a poignant light on the inevitable misunderstandings which would arise between two such widely different races. He called brandy 'the King', since this was a toast commonly and perfunctorily uttered by the officers of the garrison as they drank their liquor. As with indigenous people throughout the Pacific and the Americas, 'the King' was to be a lasting plague amongst the native peoples of the Australian continent. The lags of London's Tottenham Court Road and the West Country lacked any inhibitions also about passing syphilis on to the 'Indians'.

As had happened in Mexico, the native people sometimes showed a fatal fascination or bemusement in the face of the fallen stars. The most famous Aboriginal 'ambassador' captured on the north side of the harbour, Bennelong, was ultimately to travel to England with Phillip and be given a coat by George III. But through leaving his tribal ground for such a time and such a distance Bennelong lost his tribal virtue and his tribal wife. He ended his days as a pensioner of the state, dependent on rations and liquor, in a hut on the point where the Opera House now stands. He was a victim both of the King and of 'the King'. It could be said that his life encapsulates the sad history of his people during the next hundred years and beyond.

Though a severe famine had struck the far penal planet called New South Wales, the unknowing British government showed its determination to persevere with transportation by sending a Second Fleet in 1790 and then a Third. Conditions on the Second Fleet rivalled the worst barbarities of slave transportation from Africa and of other sinister transportations which occurred throughout the twentieth century in eastern Europe. It has to be said, though, that the British governments who were to preside over transportation for the next eighty years did not cynically take the attitude of 'Kill them on the boats or land them half dead on the distant shore, but just get rid of them.' Much thought was given to ensuring that ship-owners did not profit by letting convicts die aboard and then selling the saved convict stores at an inflated price ashore in Sydney.

The system of course had its bureaucrats, and it is through them that a great deal is known about the convicts. You cannot look at these records without feeling the poignancy, and perhaps an over-sentimental identification with the undistinguished list of ordinary names and trades and the massiveness of the sentences. The Georgian bureaucrats didn't always manage to despatch the records at the same time as they despatched the convicts. There was a case of Irish convicts who arrived in 1800 and whose records arrived in 1818. But generally – if you know where to look – you can find the name of the convict, the age, the trade, the crime, the length of the sentence, where they were tried,

Above: 'There was much about the Australian landscape that baffled the European mind.' Bush country near Koorooman, Victoria
Right: 'As on all frontiers, you made use of what was there.' An early settler in his bark shanty

Macquarie, the first army man to be appointed to the task, broke this tyrannous control. He founded a number of inland towns, and saw New South Wales as having a future more promising than that of a mere prison colony. It could be argued that perhaps the greatest monument to his administration is associated with the Governor's dining room, with the table itself, because in 1810 he invited to his table four ex-convicts or Emancipists as they were called. One was a forger; one a former mutineer from the Royal Navy called William Redfern; and the other two were thieves. As well as having dinner with Emancipists, Macquarie appointed some of them magistrates, Redfern included. The Exclusives – as the scattering of free settlers and former garrison officers called themselves – never forgave him for breaking bread with former lags. They considered that the highest table in the settlement had been stained by felon hands.

From that point on they refused to dine with him, and for the next quarter of a century they lobbied the British government to subvert the emergence of all democratic institutions in Australia. They wanted a future in which an endless supply of low-cost convict labour and depressed, time-served criminals provided the muscle; there were plenty of Spanish colonial precedents for this sort of society. But Macquarie, though a viceroy of limited upbringing, bravely insisted on setting Australia on the egalitarian path that was already there, inherent in its genes.

One of his worst opponents in the later part of his Australian career was John Macarthur, the first importer of Merino sheep into the country and hailed in history books and on the $2 note as the founder of the Australian wool industry. Lobbied by Macarthur and others, the British government sent the Chief Justice of the slave colony of Trinidad, John Thomas Bigge, as a royal commissioner to investigate Macquarie's behaviour. Lord Bathurst, the Home Secretary, had virtually told Bigge what he wanted the findings of the royal commission to be. In a famous phrase, he said that he wanted convict transportation to be looked upon by British criminals as 'an object of real terror'. The success and social standing of convicts like Henry Kable, William Redfern, the tycoon Simeon Lord and the merchant Mary Reiby did not seem to fit with Lord Bathurst's idea that transportation should equal extinction.

Opposite above: Caged prisoners on a transport bound for Australia

Opposite below: 'Melbourne, the Promised Land' reads a poster behind these emigrants. From the 1840s Australia developed a new image as a place in which to make one's fortune. The shepherd with his sheepdog was well fitted to do so

After twelve years in office, Governor Macquarie was recalled. And yet during his time in New South Wales the picture of Australia was altered beyond recognition in the minds of people everywhere. For a quarter-century after the first settlement, the imperfect society of New South Wales was strung out along the coast. There were also two small penal settlements on the beautiful island of Van Diemen's Land. But inland from Sydney rose the coastal mountains – the Blue Mountains as they were called. Whenever I holidayed there as a child, I always found it hard to understand why they had seemed such a barrier in those first few decades. But the gorges were not negotiable, it seems, and the sudden escarpments of sandstone were unclimbable.

Above: The Port Arthur model penal settlement in Tasmania as it appears today. In the nineteenth century flogging was replaced here by a sophisticated and mind-destroying form of solitary confinement.

Right: Black-eyed Sue and Sweet Poll of Plymouth take leave of their lovers, who are being transported to Botany Bay

Governors may not have wanted the mountains crossed, specifically because they provided a potential way out for the prisoner. Some of the less educated of the early convicts believed that China lay beyond them, and many a poor mugger or shoplifter set out from Sydney to try to work his way through them and find the court of the Manchus and the mercies of some Chinese princess. It is hard to get the atmosphere of such desperation as you sit at Mount Victoria or Katoomba, two tourist towns in the Blue Mountains, eat a Devonshire cream tea and look at the great sandstone walls which once stood as the barrier between the penal universe and the glories of Cathay.

In 1813 there was drought along the coast and a lack of pasturage for the flocks and herds of both Emancipists and Exclusives. And the map itself must have teased the lively minds of people like Macquarie, because the coastline of the continent had now been entirely charted by an energetic young naval officer called Matthew Flinders, who had proved that Australia was indeed a continent and not a string of islands. This tragic young man, who was to be a prisoner of the French for some years and was to die too young, is often credited – through his great work on Australian navigation – with having coined the term 'Australia'. From about the end of the Napoleonic Wars this name would overtake the older titles – New South Wales, Botany Bay, New Holland.

In any case, early in Macquarie's governorship three young men of the colony believed that they could cross the mountains by following the ridges rather than trying to sort their way through the chasms. They succeeded in a mere few days, traversing an area which can still be a dangerous tangle to the trekker. Beyond the mountains they found not China but a seemingly limitless Arcadia. One of the explorers was William Charles Wentworth, the illegitimate son of a convict woman and a naval surgeon. And since the hinterland he had found by its very size contradicted the idea of containment, of penal settlement, it seems appropriate that he had been suckled at the breast of a convict girl.

In the years after the breakout a number of exploring parties crossed the barrier and found rivers which flowed west into the interior. I have already made the point that there was much about the Australian landscape which baffled the European mind. But these rivers were at first thought to promise something very satisfying to the European consciousness – a great inland sea. Eventually Australia, beautiful in its own strange right and unfussed over anyone's expectations, would show this expectation too to be false.

After the crossing, Macquarie and later Governors had an enormous territory to administer with inadequate colonial bureaucrats. Excluding what would later become Western Australia, Macquarie had theoretical control over the two million square miles of the eastern part of the continent. So he drew twenty counties along the coast. Those who went beyond them went beyond government jurisdiction and could not claim title to any land they occupied. People did, however, go over the mountains and far beyond the twenty counties. Such pastures were out there!

In American westerns, the sheep man is always a timid and under-gunned opponent of the cattle man. But in Australia sheep were the focus of the European dreaming and the basis of the greatest fortunes. For the great woollen mills of Bradford, Halifax and Huddersfield were voracious for wool, and the Australian staple was just right in length and texture for the new machines. A British industrialist could get wool from Sydney or Hobart just as cheaply as from the traditional areas of supply like Saxony, Austria and Spain, and with far greater security of supply.

Those with a little capital and initiative would buy Merino sheep in Sydney, hire shepherds – generally ex-convicts – load up the drays and travel hundreds of miles into an interior which they looked upon as trackless. When they came to an area to which no other Briton was at that moment making claim, they ran their flocks on that land. It was land to which, under the twenty counties idea, they had no legal title, and hence they became known as 'squatters'.

It didn't matter if you were the illegitimate son of an Irish convict or the younger son of a good English family – the Australian frontier imposed the same harsh terms on everyone. The gamble was on again. And again Australia refused to fit in exactly with the squatters' intentions. There would always be cycles of drought. When it rained it would often rain a flood. Dangerous fires swept the landscape. There was pestilence amongst the livestock. There were fluctuating market prices, too. And there were many small, bloody, largely unrecorded clashes with the tribespeople. For their spirit places, the places to which their souls returned after death, often coincided with the best waterholes along rivers.

And again, whoever you were, you faced at the start of your pastoral career the same conditions of frontier squalor. As on all frontiers, you made use of what was there. Until the invention of galvanised iron later in the century – and galvanised iron would be a product the Australians would take unto themselves to the point where it became a sort of national icon – your roof was of stringy bark, a wonderfully adaptable material which had kept Aboriginals dry during storms for millennia. Now it was pressed into service to keep rain off the heads of the white settlers. Then there was the framework of logs filled in with slab timber; and, of course, the prototypical Australian veranda.

Whenever you find an old hut in the bush, even one from later in the nineteenth century, you can't help but wonder how it was for a girl from Argyll or County Clare or Dorset, when her husband brought her the great distance over from the coast and showed her such a place. And here, she knew, thirty miles or more from the nearest woman and far from civilised amenities, she would bear her children and spend the best years of her life.

The environment of the bush reinforced in its way all the traditions of the convict system – self-reliance and dependence on the few mates who surrounded you. The propaganda of settlement, expressed in the paintings of the time, stressed the danger of attacks by wild Aboriginals. More often, it would seem

Opposite: The colours of the Australian landscape were like nothing the early European settlers had ever seen before

Sydney Harbour today. 'Into this great space of harbour there drifted in late January 1788 a most remarkable flotilla of small ships'
Inset: The face of modern Sydney

Right: The Conciliation, *painted by Benjamin Duterrau.*
Far right: Hyde Park. Old Days of Cricket, *painted by T. H. Lewis*
Below right: The Eureka Stockade has become a symbol of national rebelliousness in the face of tyranny. Painting by B. Ireland
Below: Thousands of diggers homed in on places such as Ballarat and Castlemaine in the gold rush of the 1850s. Painting by E. Stocqueler

Right: Kangaroo paw, one of the exotic plants unique to Australia
Far right: A waterfall in Lamington National Park
Below: Australia's swamplands may conceal crocodiles, once hunted for their skins but now protected

on pure statistical grounds, the attack came from the other direction, from the settlers. Among the Aboriginals who did organise fierce resistance was a New South Wales tribesman, Mosquito, who was transported to Van Diemen's Land. Before mounting the gallows in 1825, he said, 'White fella soon kill all black fella....' And indeed the tribes declined for the usual New World reasons – tribespeople lacked the sort of *national* cohesion which marked the Europeans. They also had inferior weapons. But there were subtler reasons for the decline as well.

At first the squatters' flocks were cared for by night watchmen and shepherds. But the ultimate statement of European possession would be the fence. Far more than the spreading of disease, or the poisoning of flour issued to the tribespeople, or the hunting of Aboriginals as if they were game – far more than any of that, the fence interrupted the access of the tribes to the Dreaming trails and so helped wither the Aboriginal soul.

Today the Federal Land Rights Act, which for constitutional reasons operates only in the Northern Territory of Australia, enables Aboriginals to apply for excisions – the granting of access to certain sites of great importance which happen to be surrounded by the property of a pastoralist. The cattlemen don't like excisions, but the fact that they are included in the Act indicates an understanding of the impact of the fence and the European concept of property on the tribal universe.

As Aboriginal Australia began to die, the image of the continent in the minds of some Europeans continued to expand. The contradiction between Australia as a penal station on the one hand and an immensity of pastoral earth on the other began to make itself apparent to a syndicate led by a young London lawyer, Thomas Peel. He was a cousin of the then Home Secretary, Robert Peel, who was the minister in charge of convict transportation to Australia. William Peel's group negotiated a deal with the British government by which they would land free settlers and be rewarded with massive acreages – Peel himself stood ultimately to occupy a million acres, and actually staked out two hundred and fifty thousand acres on the south banks of the Swan and Canning Rivers. So the establishment of Fremantle and Perth occurred, places free of convict labour. Many settlers would leave harsh Western Australia in disgust and go elsewhere; ultimately the Western Australians had to accept convicts as a source of free labour, and continued to do so for nearly forty years.

Another young British lawyer, Edward Gibbon Wakefield, while doing time in Newgate for the attempted abduction to Gretna Green of a fifteen-year-old heiress, wrote a study of emigration to Australia. The Australian colonies, he said, were suffering from a reckless system of land granting, a great shortage of free labour and a consequent need to seek the degraded and degrading labour of convicts. He suggested that settlements be made where land could be sold at a price high enough to finance the bringing of free immigrants from Britain to provide a labour pool.

Opposite: Aborigines fishing in Arnhem Land, Northern Territory

Wakefield, like so many others who laid down the law for Australians, never visited Australia, but his plan was tried out in the St Vincent's Gulf area of South Australia in 1836. The settlement led to the making of the city of Adelaide, and though Wakefield's plan, like all perfect ones, showed unexpected human fallibilities and nearly led to colonial bankruptcy, the settlement did survive. To this day the South Australians, with something between profound seriousness and joviality, congratulate themselves on their non-convict origins. The idea that many released convicts from Tasmania and New South Wales may have emigrated there and infected the South Australian stock is ignored.

Meanwhile a curious and illicit settlement had begun at Port Phillip. It would in time become the great Victorian city of Melbourne, but for the moment it was settled without authorisation on behalf of a group of Tasmanian graziers who had heard about it from various sealing captains. When the Port Phillip area became an official settlement in 1839, it also depended – like most other areas of the continent – on convict labour.

Probably more than half the convicts worked either for government as clerks and labourers or as assigned servants to farmers, who might themselves be free immigrants or time-served lags. But the irony of this immense outdoor prison, as with Siberia, is that there had to be places of secondary punishment, and even tertiary, short of death. If a convict in Sydney or Hobart committed a further crime, where was he to be put?

In the spirit of this question, a secondary penal settlement was begun on the Hunter River in New South Wales, where there were coal deposits. Coal-mining seemed an apposite, dirty and dangerous punishment. Port Macquarie, now a coastal resort town, and Moreton Bay – which would become Brisbane – were both places of secondary and often bitter punishment. A great deal of informal exploration was done by convicts escaping from Moreton Bay and heading south, and by others escaping from Port Macquarie and heading north. Returning at last in desperation from their attempted escapes, they would give accounts of the land they had crossed in the hope of lightening the toll of lashes they would have now to bear.

Of course, there had always been Norfolk Island, that wonderful little volcanic rock way out in the Pacific which had fallen into disuse for a time but was revivified in 1825 with the express intention of making it a hell-hole. And there was a frightful, rainswept port on the west coast of Van Diemen's Land called Macquarie Harbour. But the place which symbolises the apogee of the convict system is Port Arthur in Van Diemen's Land or – as its citizens would choose to call it from 1855, as if to erase the memory of the system's savageries – Tasmania. Port Arthur lies on the beautiful and grand Tasman peninsula, which is connected to the mainland by a minute neck of land named Eaglehawk. This was patrolled by guards, and by savage dogs placed just far enough from each other to prevent them from devouring themselves, but close enough to catch the escapee.

Beginning in 1830, Port Arthur and its surrounding stations slowly took on the look of the grandeur of justice – the sort of grandeur you see in Kilmainham Gaol, Dublin. So great Victorian buildings stood amongst the quintessentially Australian beauties of one of the most exquisite parts of the continent. There were seven grades of Vandemonian convict, and only those amongst the lower grades or political prisoners came here. If, for example, you had tried to start a trade union, as had George Lovelace, the Tolpuddle Martyr who tried to found an agricultural union in Dorset and took an illegal oath by so doing, then you could be sent here or at least witness its horrors. If you were involved in a republican movement in Canada, like eighteen-year-old Linus Miller, this is where you came. The treatment comprised a strange mixture of enlightenment and savagery. A leader of the Young Ireland movement, William Smith O'Brien, refused to give his word of honour that he would not attempt to escape; he was sent here but allowed to live in his own cottage. On the other hand – and from the same period – we have accounts of Port Arthur criminals who received during the term of their sentences three thousand lashes or more. Many humbler Irish rebels than Smith O'Brien suffered here, as did graduates of Oxford and Cambridge, former officers of the best regiments, and a soldier who fell asleep on guard duty in Barbados. Here, according to official policy, especially under Lieutenant-Governor George Arthur whose evangelical severity towards convicts would fuel the prison reforming work of the Molesworth Committee back in Britain, convicts saw the system's cruellest face.

Towards the end of the practice of transportation to Van Diemen's Land, the system was brought to a curious limit at the model prison of Port Arthur. According to a plan already devised and put into practice at Pentonville Prison in London, and in a sincere attempt to avoid the relentless flogging of recidivists, a sophisticated structure was put up in which the convict was subject to the deprivation of the senses and of all human contact and affection. This place was reserved for political and criminal intransigents. Orders were given by the light tinkling of a bell. Guards wore felt shoes. Prisoners were not permitted to talk to anyone, even in the exercise yard, where to hide their features from the world they were forced to wear masks. It might be thought that in chapel there would be some relaxation of this regimen: but on the contrary, here the thoroughness of the system was taken to a further extreme. Prisoners were directed to their pew by guards who showed each a number and a letter. When a prisoner was in place, he was separated from his fellow prisoners on either side by doors. The prisoners to right and left, above and below, were all invisible. Only the chaplain could be seen. Except in his cell, where he worked on a weaving machine or on picking coir, and in the sight of God where he might or might not utter his prayers, a prisoner was faceless.

In Tasmania, as on the mainland, attacks were now made on the convict system. Australians did not wish to continue into history with the imputation that they were of felon stock. In fact the avoidance of such an imputation would

Towns like Ballarat owed their entire existence to the gold rush
Below: The Chinese cemetery at Beechworth, with two ceremonial burning towers in the foreground. On the goldfields the Chinese were often only allowed to rework alluvium discarded by European diggers

take up a lot of their mental and nervous energy for a long time yet. Most of the squatters wanted convict labour to continue to arrive, for it helped them to keep wages down. But free settlers and merchants wanted it to end for exactly the same reason. High prices for labour meant a robust commercial community. When the British government, specifically its Secretary for the Colonies, William Gladstone, sent two convict ships, *Hashemy* and *Randolph*, in answer to the demands of squatters for more labour, the citizens of Sydney and then those of Melbourne refused to receive them. Statements reminiscent of American republicanism were made at public meetings opposing the landing of convicts.

One such statement was uttered in Sydney by Henry Parkes, a young ivory turner from Birmingham recently turned populist colonial politician. (Later in the century he would propose the federation of the Australian states.) It was demeaning, said Parkes, for a nation to take the criminal detritus of another country. In Tasmania there was agitation to end the system which so dominated and marred Vandemonian society that even today the delightful city of Hobart still seems torn between a desire to embrace the future and a tendency to be consumed by its gothic convict past.

But certain modest events in the wilderness would soon not only make the debate over convictism irrelevant. They would also give new definition to the future of Australia as a place of European prosperity.

On a hot day in February 1851 a young man called Edward Hargraves, recently back from the goldfields in California, panned for gold along Lewis Ponds Creek near Bathurst in New South Wales. He was very much a gambler in the narrow sense – the sort of man who wants heaven to fall on him without his meriting it much. When he found some gold in the bottom of his pan, he spoke like a pools winner. 'I shall be a baronet,' he informed his companion. 'You will be knighted, and my old horse will be stuffed, put into a glass case, and sent to the British Museum.' The results for him personally would not be so sublime. The results for Australia would be incalculable.

I have occasionally felt that gold virus in a small way myself, that fever which would populate Australia in the 1850s, when I've bent down to the water of some stream, sluicing water through the gravel in the pan in the hope that grains of gold, in all their glory and weight, will sink to the bottom. It is only an echo, however, of the impact that the daily lottery of sluicing gravel and finding wealth in the corner of a pan had on the imaginations of nineteenth-century Europeans and Asians.

Gold had been discovered in New South Wales in the 1830s and 1840s, but there had been two strong reasons why the news had never got out. One was that by British law all precious metals found in British colonies belonged to the Crown: there was therefore no incentive for seekers or entrepreneurs to go after the stuff. The second reason, and perhaps the more important, was that

A digger and his mates pose, probably for a travelling photographer, outside the entrance to a gold mine

47

*'The fraternal tra-
dition of the convict
gang and the remote
farm'* – a scene on a
New South Wales
bush property in the
1890s

the colonial governors sat on the news because they feared it would unsettle the convicts, that it would cause them to bolt for inland creeks, and that even the labouring classes would leave their shepherding or their trades in the cities and do likewise.

In 1849 there was a gold rush in California, however, and many free Australian labourers went off to that in any case, creating a labour shortage just at the time when New South Wales and the Port Phillip district (which would soon become known as Victoria) had renounced convict transportation as a source of labour. When Hargraves and his colleagues returned from America they brought back not only the method of panning, but also the device known as the cradle, an extension of the pan. It was indeed shaped like a wooden cradle with a handle on top. Alluvium was shovelled into the top of it, water was poured in at the top, and then there were a series of sieves. Nuggets would deposit themselves in a tray, and gold grains would accumulate on the lowest ledge. All else, being lighter, would ultimately be rocked and washed out.

More excitingly, there was always the chance of simply digging up a nugget, or tripping over one. Two sailors jumped ship in Melbourne in 1853, walked north to Castlemaine and, on the gravelly banks of some creek, dug up out of a small claim two hundredweight of gold within a few days. This was the sort of story which reached the British, European and American press and brought the boatloads. In the face of such a rush of seekers any ancient fictions about Crown ownership of gold found in the bush seemed to evaporate. And the pan and cradle of course made convictism finally impossible. A British official remarked, 'Where is the sense in shipping convicts to an area to which free men are clamouring to go at their own expense?' Within ten years Melbourne was transformed from a pastoral village to a booming and then a grand Victorian city. The potency of gold can be seen, too, in such places as Ballarat and Bendigo and Castlemaine and Beechworth, with the solidity of their public buildings, their cathedrals, their Masonic temples and their schools of art.

The seekers called themselves diggers, and the name was to stick. They were gamblers on the grand scale and had often abandoned wives, property and professional prospects to beat their way to a forlorn creek in the Australian wilderness and dig their way down from one layer of gravel to another. There was, however, an economic law of which the diggers seemed to be ignorant: that the more gold they dug up, the higher the price of everything – flour, shovels, tents and shirts – became.

The old tradition of dependence on a mate – the fraternal tradition of the convict gang and the remote farm, later to be criticised by feminists as the wellspring of Australian sexism – was strengthened here. Some men brought their wives with them or found 'mates' in the stricter sense amongst the local girls. But generally it was a matter of two men – one below to do the digging, one above to do the sluicing. Unless, of course, some great gold rock revealed itself dully in the narrow pit – then the digger and his mate departed by coach to Melbourne, scattering £5 notes behind them, and ill-prepared by the air of recklessness at the diggings for hanging on to their fortune in the end. It would be in commercial mining, when the alluvial gold gave out, that the fortunes would be made.

These old fields are silent and haunted now. The bush has regrown over them, but they are so pockmarked with the energy of those vanished miners that it is often still dangerous to walk around too freely. You can encounter water sluices dug in the ground and lined with sandstone, and little cunning stone chimneys where some artful Cornishman agreed to smelt the stuff down for the other diggers for a percentage. And you keep on encountering the most pitiable ghosts. In a sheep pasture near Castlemaine, for example, stand a few graves of Chinese diggers. The Chinese called Australia New Gold Mountain, as distinct from the Old Gold Mountain of California. They were discriminated against on the diggings and often permitted only to rework the alluvium the European diggers had already worked through. When they fell, their comrades buried them very close by, but – it would appear – with ceremony, since the grave markers are of stone and the names are in Chinese script. There is a much bigger Chinese graveyard near the old gold town of Beechworth. The Chinese had come to remind the Australians that, though the Australian soul might consider itself European, the Australian location was Asian. That contradiction still teases Australian society and generates plentiful debate late in the twentieth century, just as it did in the nineteenth.

But perhaps most poignant of all is the graveyard of the children of diggers, consumed by an 1854 cholera epidemic in the gold town of Forrest Creek in Victoria. Forrest Creek was a characteristic rush. One month there was nobody here but tribal Aboriginals, the next twenty thousand avid seekers. The children are buried under arduously made gravestones on a hill called Pennyweight – obviously because it was not gold-bearing country in any substantial way, and so the children would not be disturbed by later gold hunger. 'John,' says one of the gravestones. 'Beloved son, died 11 September, 1854, aged 10 months.' On the flats below this graveyard now lies a village of perhaps two hundred people.

The great popular gold rush had a potent political influence. It was attended by Prussian intellectuals and conscientious objectors, by forthright Americans, by Italian nationalists, by Chartists, by disciples of the founder of the Co-operative movement, Robert Owen, and of course by the disinherited Irish, many of them with strong political instincts. And all of them picked up the stench of ancient tyranny in the practices surrounding the gold licence.

The licence required the digger to pay only a little less over a year than a squatter would, the squatter running sheep on an area of perhaps twelve miles by twelve miles or more, the digger to be restricted to a mere twelve feet by twelve feet. While the alluvial gold was plentiful, the diggers didn't particularly mind paying these fees – they remained speculators, that is, and not politicians.

Right: A miner panning for gold in Western Australia – 'the daily lottery of sluicing gravel and finding wealth'

Opposite above: The tyranny of the gold licence, and its savage enforcement by corrupt police, led to revolt among the gold diggers

Opposite below: A group of miners at Brady's Gully, Tee-tulpa goldfields, South Australia, photo-graphed in 1886

DOWN WITH THE LICENSE FEE!
DOWN WITH DESPOTISM!
"WHO SO BASE AS BE A SLAVE?"

ON

WEDNESDAY NEXT

The 20th Instant, at Two o'clock,

A MEETING

Of all the DIGGERS, STOREKEEPERS, and Inhabitants of Ballarat generally, will be held

ON BAKERY HILL

For the immediate Abolition of the License Fee, and the speedy attainment of the other objects of the Ballarat Reform League. The report of the Deputation which have gone to the Lieutenant-Governor to demand the release of the prisoners lately convicted, and to Creswick and Forest Creeks, Bendigo, &c, will also be submitted at the same time.

All who claim the right to a voice in the framing of the Laws under which they should live, are solemnly bound to attend the Meeting and further its objects to the utmost extent of their power.

N.B. **Bring your Licenses, they may be wanted.**

But as gold got rarer, and the shafts had to be sunk more deeply, the licences and their expense became a matter of resentment – especially as the diggers had no representation in colonial legislatures. The Americans had a tried formula for this situation – 'No Taxation without Representation'. Refugees from the European revolutions of 1848 added their philosophical objections to the nature of colonial politics. The gold licence was enforced tyrannously by the mounted police, known as the traps. Their style involved bodily savagery, the use of firearms and perjury. Everything they did on the goldfields reinforced that Australian mistrust for uniformed authority which had begun with convictism and which would express itself ultimately in strange forms in the idiosyncratic Australian armed forces of two world wars.

The diggers, amongst them an Irishman called Peter Lalor and a disciple of Garibaldi called Raffaello Carboni, created a Reform League at Ballarat and demanded the franchise. They flew a flag based on the Southern Cross and they raised a stockade at a place called Eureka, a field where gold-seekers had to dig to a great depth to find the gold reefs, and where therefore the sense of grievance against the licence was strongest. The colonial governor was a naval officer called Hotham. Unaccustomed to the democratic enthusiasms of the age and fearing an American-style revolution, he called on troops from other colonies and sent redcoats marching towards Ballarat.

It was soldiers from a Somerset regiment who were actually engaged in the assault on the Eureka Stockade in the dawn of 3 December 1854. The forces of British order now lay face to face with the anger of the Irish, the rugged democracy of the Yankees and the Chartist belief in the dignity of man. In a chaotic spate of hand-to-hand fighting, up to thirty diggers were killed.

The potential of the event in terms of the British Empire on one side and Australian democracy on the other was far greater than the brief mayhem that Sunday morning. The location of the Eureka Stockade is not known to the nearest yard, and that is characteristic. Australians, very good rebels, are none the less half-embarrassed by revolution itself. The flag which flew at Eureka stands on the blind side of a stairwell in the Ballarat Art Museum – to save it from damage by sun, the curators say. But one cannot help but think it, amongst Ballarat's charming but sometimes ordinary collection, strangely placed.

But wherever the stockade stood, there is no doubt where Eureka stands in Australian legend and history: its position is dead centre. In legend it is a case of a group of Australians (very few of them native-born, but we can let that stand) imbued with passionate concepts of democracy and fighting for that most Australian of birthrights, the Fair Go. The Fair Go has always been invoked in the streets, the workshops, the Parliaments. It is like an unwritten constitution. And what it means in general terms is natural justice based never on ideology but always on practical equality: 'Socialism without ideas', as one French visitor put it.

Like many other bloody little colonial skirmishes, such as the battle at

*Left: 'By the 1860s the country was ... becoming the world's most advanced bourgeois democracy.' The reading room in Melbourne Public Library
Below: 'In nearly every town a Mechanics' Institute or a School of Arts was built.' The Gordon Institute of Technology, Geelong*

Concord Bridge, Massachusetts, in 1776, Eureka had a potent political impact. Just how powerful is still argued; but it is true that within a year of the fight here miners' licences had been abolished and miners' courts had been set up to deal with questions of mining rights. And within two or three years four of the five then Australian colonies – Queensland had not yet separated from New South Wales – had introduced the franchise for all adult males, long before the British, long before nearly any other nation.

The Eureka flag is flown still. It is a symbol to those who wish for an Australian republic: from Eureka onwards that question would be a live one. It is flown by militant trade unionists, too. You might also see it waved on the hill at Sydney during Test matches. It expresses that other side of the Australian character, the side which is not loyalist. The other side, you could say, of the Australian soul – since, as many observers point out, you will often find conservatism and rebellion in the one person.

The Eureka side of the Australian soul involved a scepticism about authority and a forthright demand for a fair, even a utopian, society. The idea was that it made little sense to make the enormous journey to Australia if you were going to cop the same nonsense there as you did back home in Europe. And despite the increasing numbers of women emigrating to Australia, many of them through schemes initiated by the remarkable Caroline Chisholm, the ultimate domestic Australian virtue was all to do with sticking by your mates, a robust ethic which would give wings to the early trade union movement but from which women and Aboriginals were often excluded.

And what about the intellect? It would always be fashionable to consider Australians as something like the Texans of the South Seas – mere bush barbarians. But by the 1860s the country was in fact becoming the world's most advanced bourgeois democracy, and the Australians themselves were avid for self-improvement. In nearly every town a Mechanics' Institute or a School of Arts was built, where the artisan, the shearer, the miner could improve himself by access to the ideas of the age through lectures and debates and libraries. Libraries, like the still extant one which lies under the Ballarat Mechanics' Institute, featured such works as *Inquiries into Truth, Communistic Societies in the United States, Rule and Misrule of the English and America, The Diffusion of Knowledge,* and the works of Hobbes, Adam Smith, Hegel, de Tocqueville and so on. Such reading fed directly into the lively debates going on in society at large concerning trade unionism and the eight-hour day (the industrial version of the Fair Go), compensation for workers' injury and a half day off on Saturday. Australians are rather chagrined that no one knows that these reforms were achieved in their mere colonies earlier than they were in nearly any independent country in the world.

Eight-hour day! For the Australian worker, as for the convict long before him, his own time, when he was no longer required to answer his master's demands, was the most sacred time of all. And perhaps there is still no other

Opposite above: A boating party was an elegant form of relax-ation for better-off Australians at the turn of the century

Opposite below: Leisure time has always been highly regarded in Australia, and cricket is still a national obsession. The Australian team of 1886

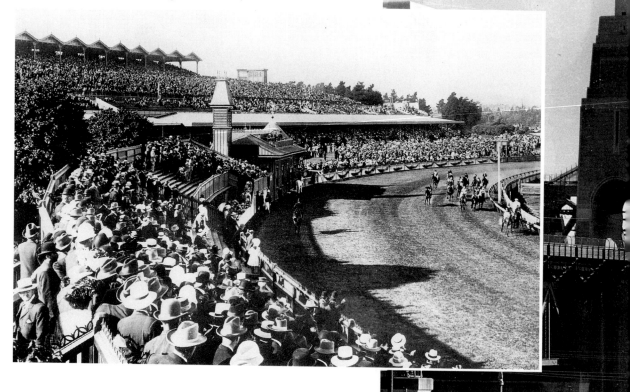

Below: 'Immense stakes go down on horse races.' An early twentieth-century meeting at Flemington racecourse, Melbourne

Right: On a sun-soaked Saturday afternoon bowlers concentrate on their game under the famous silhouette of Sydney Harbour Bridge

'Gambling pervades the Australian weekend.' A thirties' aerial view of an illegal game of two-up

nation on earth so devoted to its leisure, no other nation where the weekend is so sacrosanct and inviolable. Those Australians in the service industries who have to work at weekends are often compensated with double pay for their great sacrifice. Service is not seen as the road to Puritan redemption and wealth, as is the New England tradition. Service (often admittedly genial and generous) is rather something exceptional to expect of a fellow free citizen, and is worthy of special rewards at the industrial level.

Gambling pervades the Australian weekend, as it pervaded that late Georgian era from which the first unwilling emigrants derived. Immense stakes go down on horse races. Vast crowds attend football matches in the winter, especially Australian Rules, a derivative of Gaelic football, which is popular in most Australian states. In every suburb there are bowling greens, so that even grandmothers find their own sun-drenched recreation in the rather coy uniforms of the bowling clubs. In the summer the sea is cherished and the sand perhaps a little more so. Surf carnivals are held – the surf boats of various clubs compete against each other in turbulent seas. There are surf-ski races which involve such energy that you begin to think that leisure is perhaps the most vigorous of all national industries. There is also of course always cricket, and a good hook, late cut, cover drive relieves all cosmic anxieties. Why shouldn't it? And under their frank sun Australians at leisure, tending their barbecues and listening to the latest score or racing odds, tend to mutter the Antipodean versions of *mañana* – 'She'll be right!' (the 'she' being the state of the known universe) and 'No worries!'

Much of Australia is amongst the oldest land surface in the world; the oldest daughter of that ancient landmass, mother of all the continents, Pangaea. You do not have to seek far into the interior of Australia before this antiquity strikes and humbles you. This place, you feel, has seen everything, and you have seen little. This country, having its own wisdom and its own cycles – it will do for you if you make too many presumptions of it.

On the ancient soil of Australia the squatter – who got there first – had early understood that it was best to be big if you wanted to succeed. That hypothetical girl from Argyll or County Clare or Dorset who set up home under a stringy bark roof with her squatter husband might well, within twenty or thirty years, have been presented by King Wool with a fortune that enabled them to build one of those bush chateaux which you still encounter, tastefully screened by imported stands of trees, on Australian back roads; houses often as grand as or grander than anything King Cotton built in the South of the United States.

The squatters were generally conservative, Anglophile. In the midst of breathless Australian summers they expressed in their expensive household decorations an understandable nostalgia for the northern hemisphere, but also a passionate attachment to the Antipodean spaces they occupied. Their position had been regularised by now, so that they owned some of their property freehold, leasing further great stretches for negligible sums. Having originally occupied the new world without government authorisation, some of them now tended to think they owned it by divine right.

As the alluvial gold gave out, diggers and other immigrants began to cry for the unlocking of the land. So did theorists and politicians. For surely Australia was meant to be something other than one enormous sheep walk. A member of the Victorian Legislative Assembly, Charles Gavan Duffy – later Sir Charles, and Chief Justice of Victoria, but also a former rebel of the Young Ireland movement – was just one of those who campaigned through the Victorian Land League for the proposition of breaking the hold of the squatter over the soil of Australia. In the Legislative Council of New South Wales, the liberal-minded John Robertson argued with the squatters about setting up yeoman-style farmers in the bush.

A number of selection acts were passed in the legislatures of various of the Australian colonies. Ordinary folk were permitted to 'select' up to a square mile of land, including land that the squatters had up till then occupied on leasehold. The squatters used a number of ruses to keep the best leasehold land under their control – such as the use of 'dummy' claimants who 'selected' land apparently on their own behalf but secretly on the squatter's. But suddenly, and on whatever onerous terms, the bush was full of selector farmers – the cockatoo or cocky farmers, as they would become known in the Australian idiom. They were to increase land under cultivation in Australia sevenfold.

Often the land they selected was unsuitable for the intensive farming that the first land reformers had envisaged. It was the selector, however, who in popular art and literature became the Australian hero. The marginal selector was honoured as the 'battler'. To call a man a 'battler' even today is still to honour him. Battlers are those who, in pursuing very modest dreams, face a predestined defeat, generally at the hands of mortgages and cycles of flood, drought and fire. They are admired for their vanquished courage, since it is courage and not success which is the object of worship to Australians.

Whether destined to become battlers or not, immigrants were staggered in those first years of selection to be able to occupy acreages that they could never have thought of owning in their countries of origin. And this was particularly true of a race which carried in their blood an ancient land hunger – the Irish. One such family, named Kelly, settled on a back road in the north-east of Victoria in the 1870s and ultimately became the most famous family of small Australian selectors. It happens that across the road from them another Irish family found a selection, and this family's name was Keneally, and they came from Cork. Their travails are forgotten, however; but not the travails of their famous next-door neighbour, the widow Ellen Kelly. Her late husband had been an Irish convict who had done time in Tasmania and dug for gold in Victoria. And now she settled on Lot 57A, eighty-eight acres, at East Greta in Victoria, and expected from this inadequate soil to raise her fatherless children.

As the Kelly brothers grew up they were faced with two economic choices. One was to drift away from the hut to the cities; the other was to join that vast body of itinerant Australian agricultural workers, the swagmen, which the novelist Trollope had described as one of the most remarkable institutions in any country on earth. But there was a third, illicit choice, too, one which appealed to the Kelly boys both by temperament and by race memory, and one much celebrated in Australian folksong. They could become horse thieves and cattle duffers – 'duff' being the Australian equivalent of the western American 'rustle'.

The Kellys, like many young Australians of their age, were adept bushmen. It had taken nearly a hundred years for Europeans to feel at home in the bush; the Kellys were of a generation which looked upon it as a natural environment. They had inherited the wilderness from the now scattered and demeaned tribes, and they knew how to use it for cover from the authorities. The eldest of the boys was Edward, known as Ned. He is worthy of remembrance in his own right but also, above all, because he typifies more than anyone else the strange heroes ordinary Australians would come to choose for themselves. Through his remarkable paintings the Australian artist Sidney Nolan has turned the Kelly story into a sort of Antipodean Passion and Resurrection.

The Kelly clan had been harried by squatters and police, and many of Ned's family – including his mother – had been gaoled in such places as Beechworth and Melbourne on manufactured evidence. In north-eastern Victoria, by the time Kelly had reached manhood he was in a state of revolt on the issues of both law and land, issues which echoed the causes of revolt amongst his ancestors. The events which would become known as the Kelly Outbreak were assured.

In the bush the Kellys nursed their certainty that the law was made for squatters, and planned a number of raids, demonstrations, cattle thefts and meetings with their allies on the plains. They were pursued by often inept parties of police. One such party, disguised as prospectors and sent out to ambush the Kellys, were themselves ambushed in what the Kellys described as a 'confused gun battle'. Three policemen were killed, all of them Irish like the Kellys themselves. Their gravestones and memorial sit in the cemetery in the hill town of Mansfield in Victoria. The stones do not mention the Kellys, however – the stonemason missed the significance that Sidney Nolan would later exploit. In fact the monument writes the gang off as 'armed criminals'.

For Kelly there was no way back now to the relative respectability of mere cattle duffing. Over the next few years he carried out a number of stylish bank robberies; in fact he captured entire townships. And these enterprises were managed with such panache – with the quality which is known and revered in the bush as 'flashness' – that his reputation was augmented beyond measure. He was the hero of the battlers, and behind him lay the whole question of Australian land law and bush democracy.

The icon of the legend of Ned Kelly was the iron helmet which, with its accompanying body armour, he wore at the siege of Glenrowan, a small Victorian country town. The gang had attempted to derail there a police train crowded with constables. Now they were surrounded in a pub. Kelly sympathisers have always seen this helmet and armour as indications of the limits to which one young Irish-Australian was driven by land hunger and police persecution. And indeed, at the time of the Outbreak the hills around Glenrowan were full of armed and mounted Kelly sympathisers. Ned broke his way out of the pub and went up into the hills to tell them that a general uprising was no longer possible. He was on his way back down through the paddocks in the morning mist to join his friends in the pub when he was shot in the legs and other unprotected parts, and fell with twenty-eight bullet holes in his body.

This, in some ways – though it was not quite the end of Ned Kelly – signalled the end of a growing practical republicanism in the bush. The Australians, while never forgetting him, have not known quite what to do with him. The sites of the Kelly saga go totally unmarked by plaques or marked trails. Glenrowan is now a sad little town amongst melancholy hills, full of Kelly kitsch-iana. But it is true that in the imaginations of many Australians, not least in Sidney Nolan's, Ned's fall has reverberated since that day. I have taken the liberty of telling the Ned Kelly story, as Nolan has of painting it, because it is an eloquent case history involving besetting Australian considerations – vast land and land hunger, the Irish and the English in the South Seas, bush loyalism and bush republicanism.

But even if you look on Ned as just another outlaw, then you have to say about him the same sort of things which are said of American outlaws. The railway station at Glenrowan figures a great deal in the photographs taken on the day of the siege at the Glenrowan pub. By now there was an extensive railway system, particularly in the east, built and managed by the colonial governments because private investors could not be attracted to run lines through the vast, sparsely peopled bush. The railway itself was one of the reasons that the horseman Kelly's flashness could not last. Appropriately, too, it was in the station-master's office that the much wounded Kelly, the fallen young Celtic chief, lay while in the pub his lieutenants returned the fire of the besieging police.

At last the pub was set on fire. When the body of one of Kelly's brothers was retrieved the primal keening of the Irish filled the Australian bush, and the gentlemen who posed by the coffins of two of the gang in front of Glenrowan's second pub celebrated the restoration of Anglo-Saxon authority over what they saw as wanton Irish anarchy.

Ned was nursed back to health and tried by an elegant Ulsterman called Redmond Barry. Yet even before the death sentence was pronounced official enquiries were being held into further land reform and police persecution. Kelly

Opposite right: 'The icon of the legend of Ned Kelly was the iron helmet which, with its accompanying body armour, he wore at the siege of Glenrowan

Opposite below: Ned Kelly's mother and his brother James at their home in East Greta

Above: Ludwig Leichhardt who mysteriously disappeared while trying to cross Australia from east to west

Above: 'By the 1880s ... the interior of the continent had been nearly fully defined by European explorers, who had found it a furnace and a crucible.' Detail from Burke and Wills at Mount Hopeless, *a watercolour by George Lambert*

Below: Donald Gregory Blaxland, discoverer of the Blue Mountain Pass

had made his impact. It was this relative flexibility of institutions in Australia which was part of the reason why Australians were never moved to the sort of revolution which had prevailed in America a hundred years before.

After his trial Ned was brought back to Melbourne Gaol to await execution. He would remain a curious demi-god to the growing urban working class, to many of the small selectors, to the swagmen and the shearers. But above all he represented what was becoming, rightly or wrongly, the Australian style. This involved a great personal courage, and Ned was the prototype for the laconic fatalism of the Australian army at Gallipoli some thirty-five years later.

For here in Melbourne Gaol Ned's demand was: 'Tell them I died game', a cry which would represent the Australian equivalent of *machismo* for the nation's soldiers in wars not yet envisaged. On the morning of 11 November 1880 Ned was brought to the gallows. He was only twenty-five years old. With only a few seconds to live, he murmured: 'Such is life.' And these words too would appeal to his fellow-countrymen as a sort of fatalistic creed. When the executioner pulled the lever, Ned's body dropped eight feet, the neck broken but the myth totally unimpaired.

It is curious that Australians have always favoured that species of hero who goes down inevitably against outlandish odds but who does it with style. This expectation of inevitable failure, the stress on elegant courage, is something the Australians have taken directly from the Irish character. Yet neither in landscape nor society was Australia like Ireland, even though the Irish made a substantial impact on progressive politics in Australia. Australia was a country rich in resources, and its strong suit was great social mobility for the individual. It permitted, if sometimes grudgingly, the freedom of assembly on which the early trade union movement depended, and its institutions did have some elasticity. Yet on the spiritual level Ireland and its old myths made an enormous impact and fed the national intolerance of tyranny – the reason why so many of the early settlers had arrived, freely or under duress, on those strange and unknown shores.

By the time of Kelly's death Australia was beginning to become an urban nation. The drift to the cities would be accentuated by depression and drought, the realities of Australia's economic cycles and geography. Modern Australia would become like Canada, a nation where most people lived in cities and yet maintained frontier images of themselves.

By the 1880s, too, the interior of the continent had been nearly fully defined by European explorers, who had found it a furnace and a crucible. The great Charles Sturt had thirty years past gone blind from the rigours of his search for an inland sea. The Prussian Ludwig Leichhardt, trying to cross the continent from east to west, vanished as if consumed by the earth itself. The Irishman Robert O'Hara Burke and the Englishman William Wills, ill-assorted and reckless, died at Cooper's Creek in central Australia after crossing the continent

Opposite: 'This central nature . . . contained the expectation of high living standards.' Above: In the bush people moved with their houses.

Below: Urban affluence at the turn of the century

Opposite: To the
first settlers the Blue
Mountains behind
Sydney represented an
impenetrable barrier

from south to north. Ironically, because of their rotten luck they are honoured in Australia far more than their more efficient and practical contemporary, John McDouall Stuart, whose name marks the modern highway north to Darwin. The Centre none the less brought blindness to Stuart as well.

Out of the horrifying journals of these men, out of the journals of such later explorers as the West Countryman, Ernest Giles, grew the myth of the Dead Heart, a Eurocentric picture of the desolation at Australia's core, one which was to plague and depress the Australian spirit. The lack of a Mississippi or a system of great lakes would be seen as the determinant of Australia's future. Concern over its enormity and its emptiness would spur a xenophobic fear of populous Asia.

By 1872, in spite of the ferocity of central Australia's climate and the resistance of desert tribes, a telegraph line crossed the continent south to north, Adelaide to Darwin. Characteristically, the first messages which were passed on along remote relay stations on the telegraph line through Alice Springs were not pious manifestos but rather requests for the latest European wool prices.

With such modern and unifying technologies came a sense that all the Australian colonists were one tribe. A fervent Scot called William Spence was working towards the foundation of Australia-wide industrial unions, and from politicians as well came the impulse towards federation. It was no frantic impulse, such as that which had created the United States, but it was a steady and practical desire and would ultimately be achieved. For by now there was such a being as the Australian, a man or woman with a certain set of expectations and cultural and spiritual habits. This central nature was seen as robust, forthright; it contained the expectation of high living standards. Doubtful whether even in this haven for the ordinary refugee social justice would be achieved in the end, the poet Henry Lawson wondered whether one day soon blood might stain the wattle. But in the central nature and expectations of the Australian character, coast to coast, lay the basis for Australia's coming nationhood.

Right: From the Eureka Stockade to Ned Kelly's last stand, and through two world wars, mateship has been part of the Australian psyche

Above right: 'Perhaps there is still no other nation on earth so devoted to its leisure.' A life-saver off duty

Below right: A Queensland stockman

74

Aerial view of Bondi beach, the
surfers' paradise

Above: One of the old-timers: a fossicker at an abandoned gold town. Photograph taken in the 1940s
Left: 'Galvanised iron ... became a sort of national icon.' A gold-mining township of the 1980s

2 The Road from Gundagai

PATSY ADAM-SMITH

My generation, born in the 1920s, still rode on the sheep's back as had the generations since the first decades of the nineteenth century. All Australians knew this, as they knew that the wealth of the land came from the country. This it was that set our poets singing as though they were galloping across limitless golden plains – as indeed some of them did do.

By the time I was born my family were railway people, and we lived beside the tracks all my young life. My father was a ganger with pick and shovel, my mother station-mistress at the isolated railway sidings. Our small house on the platform was the only building to be seen on the great arid plains that rolled away to the horizon, where it seemed to me, as a child, that the flat earth ended and all beyond was *terra incognita*.

It hadn't always been like that for my people. They had come here as free settlers, but bone-poor. Mum's forbears had left Ireland following the 1822 famine, and came to Australia after a few years in America. Dad's had been forced off the land in the west of Scotland at almost the same time as this southern land, sixteen thousand sailing miles away, was being taken up by white settlers. They became timber-men up in the mountains, while Mum's people took up land to milk cows 'beyond where anyone with sense or money would go', as Mum said of their struggling farms. The free, independent men of the timber country have traditionally disdained the time-tied cow-cockies with their smallholdings, and in return the more conservative cow-cockies warned their daughters against the 'wild, untamed mountain men'.

Opposite above: Ned Kelly, the most famous of all Australia's rebel-heroes, in The Trial, *one of Sidney Nolan's series of paintings of the outlaw's life and death*
Opposite below: The telegraph brought the continent together, but nature sometimes had the last word. Sand drifts over an old telegraph station in Western Australia

It was a grand background for a life. In those days before TV and radio – even before electricity came to our harsh lands on the edge of the outback – we talked and listened a lot. We spent cold desert nights in front of our red-gum fire, and in summer, after mirage-hot days, we sat outside watching the stars slide across the big sky and taking in the lore of our household. Stories were told and retold, embellished or honed down to polish them in the mould of all traditions. If the telling one night did not excite or interest the listeners, the next night the emphasis would be different, the timing, the tone, the silences altered. But always the core remained constant. In this way, by the time we children were conscious of telling the story ourselves we had become melded into the people, the land and the movements of the stars; time wavered, and it was as though we were taking part in events that in reality belonged to our forefathers' time. We had been part of the life of much of this new nation.

Opposite above: Bringing in the harvest in the wheatfields of South Australia, 'the clean, simple country life that Australians have always dreamed they were part of'

Opposite below: The harvest is gathered in, and the machinery is stored away for next season

> *There's a track winding back to an old-fashioned shack*
> *Along the road to Gundagai.*

So begins one of the best-known Australian songs. A simple thing with a catchy melody, it captured the hearts and minds of the country and had everyone believing they could see the gum trees growing, and the Murrumbidgee flowing, as they galloped back across the wide brown lands to their mythical birthplace,

> *Where my Daddy and Mummy are waiting for me*
> *And the pals of my childhood once more I will see;*
> *Then no more will I roam when I'm heading right for home,*
> *Along the road to Gundagai.*

The song encapsulated the clean, simple country life that Australians have always dreamed they were part of. No one wants to know that we have one of the highest urban populations in the world, with over 58 per cent of us living in the six state capitals that hug the eastern and southern coastlines. On 31 March 1901, when the first census was taken, the population was 3,773,801, and 1,342,675 Australians lived in cities even then. Today five out of six are city-dwellers. New South Wales has over 90 per cent of its people within the cities, and even Tasmania, with the greatest rural population of any of the states, still has only a quarter of its people out in the country. But who cares about facts when the heart is beating fast, and 'I love a sunburnt country, a land of rolling plains' is tripping sonorously off the tongue! Up until recent years Australia's economy was based almost entirely on rural production. This rural economy and the country people who made it possible influenced many of our social attitudes: our lore is almost entirely bound up with it.

That it is too lonely, brutal and mind-crippling, too distant to keep in touch

with modern events and trends – even with friends and loved ones – is not mentioned. It is as though a ban has been placed on anything that tells the truth about what this land is in reality and what it does to people. There are some, like me, brought up in the bush, who can now neither stay away from it nor live for long in it; we call ourselves the footloose ones – wandering, like the Flying Dutchman, awaiting a reprieve that will never come.

The other great Australian myth is what has always been called our lack of class distinction. It has pleased many people to speak of us as being egalitarian – it perhaps adds a fillip of distinction to the hypothesis that we are all tough men and women riding through the tall eucalyptus forests, cracking our whips and setting the earth a-quiver with our horses' hooves. The truth is that the worst excesses of the old world could not be shrugged off on the early ships in which many of our forbears travelled steerage for four months on their way to a new world. When they arrived they found the army already in occupation and hand-outs and favours already given. There was never any more egalitarianism here than elsewhere.

In the first few years of settlement sheep and their owners laid the foundations for both riches and disasters in Australia, not the least being the sheep farmers' disdain for their labourers. This unspoiled continent, isolated from outside *mores* and influences, offered an opportunity for harmonious union, master and man becoming partners. Instead, habits brought from the old, decaying world were exacerbated. Here, with unpaid convicts as servants for whose wellbeing he had no responsibility, the landowner was better off than the slave-owner of the southern states of America. And when convict transportation ended, many of the old attitudes were transferred to the working men. It was this contempt on the part of the Shepherd Kings for their fellow-men that most offended the ordinary settlers, who had looked across wide oceans and visualised a sensible, humane existence different from the one they were happy to leave behind.

In one way the class distinction in Australia was different from the ages-old social strata of England, and it took an Irishman to delineate it succinctly. When Charles Gavan Duffy was considering emigrating to Australia in 1851 he consulted William Smith O'Brien, brother of Lord Inchiquin and a direct descendant of Brian Boru, High King of Ireland – but at that time a political exile in Australia. 'Would there', he asked, 'be sufficient men of intellect, breeding and scholarship for a gentleman to be able to live in Australia as he was accustomed to do in Ireland?' O'Brien, a Latin and Greek scholar, replied, 'They are mainly of the yeoman class, but given a generation or two they will take upon themselves the appurtenances of gentlemen.' And they did, with the help of the golden fleece. Within two decades of the first settlement sheep walks had spread over the arable land. By the 1880s some properties could already boast an owner with three generations behind him who had provided wool for the mills of Yorkshire.

Lord Stanley, Secretary for the Colonies, believed that the squatters' influence

Opposite above: 'The other great Australian myth, is what has always been called our lack of class distinction.' The truth was rather different. A group of professional rat-catchers, photographed at the turn of the century, survey the results of their day's work

Opposite below: Digging yourself a fortune was one way to become upwardly mobile. The Post and Telegraph Office in the gold town of Kalgoorlie in the 1890s

Below: Grandfather Adams shearing by hand.
During the shearers' strike he walked the thou-
sand miles home
Bottom of page: Penning a flock
'My generation . . . still rode on the sheep's back.
. . .' Right: This early twentieth-century sheep-
shearing shed is already mechanised. Every year
itinerant shearers would travel thousands of miles
in search of work

in the colony 'out of the Legislature is very great, and in it, paramount to every other'. John Macarthur, one of the pioneers of sheep breeding in Australia, claimed to have secured the recall of the first four Governors of the colony of New South Wales. To the ordinary man these wealthy sheep-owners became known as the 'squattocracy' or, in reference to the mythical bush monster, the 'bunyip aristocracy'. Their counterparts in wealth and position in England held no more power than these men socially, legally or politically. Squatters with runs of up to a million acres naturally ruled society both in the city as well as in the surrounding countryside. In most outback areas small towns grew only with the support of the local properties. The landowner was the local justice of the peace and sat in judgment in the local courthouse, and if he didn't have a small private army equipped by himself he could call on the colonial army because he or his neighbours or friends were Members of Parliament.

Although many of the squatters lived in their magnificent town houses, their properties lay hundreds – some thousands – of miles inland, and to these the shearers had to make their way every year at their own expense. 'O! the springtime it brings on the shearing,' the old bush song goes, 'and then you will see them in droves. . . .' Up and down and across the entire land the shearers travelled for four months of the year to clip sheep. Men from the southern colonies of South Australia, Tasmania and Victoria travelled up to fifteen hundred miles to Queensland and Western Australia – on horseback, in carts, on bicycles, on camels and on foot.

On the day the shearing was to begin the overseer would line up the hundred or so men already assembled at the shed, pick those he wanted and 'bush' the others – tell them to pack their gear and get off the property. They would go quietly enough, hurrying to the next run perhaps fifty or a hundred miles away, and hoping to get there before that team was picked. Many top shearers spent a season as 'broomie', sweeping the floor of the shed, unable to secure a 'pen', referring to the penned up sheep in front of each individual shearer.

A shearer was paid piece rates – a sum for each sheep he sheared. In principle this was fair, if it hadn't been for raddling. Raddle was a lump of red chalk with which a squatter or his agent could mark a sheep he considered badly shorn and therefore not to be paid for. The shearer had no redress: the owner's decision was final. Some squatters boasted that they bought new properties with the money they made with raddle.

If a man was sacked he received no pay, irrespective of how long he had worked. Consequently many were sacked just prior to 'cut out', the end of the shearing. Even today shearing is not only highly skilled work but very exhausting; the position of the body is physically tiring, the heat of the tin shed intense, the speed and concentration so great that a man will start up at a sudden noise. Yet the living quarters were terrible, with fifty men eating, cooking and sleeping on bags of straw, in one windowless, dirt-floored room which was often right above the stinking sheep pens.

The great distances between the sheds made it difficult for the men to organise, but by 1886 a shearers' union had been formed. Their manifesto stated that membership of a union would make a man a better father, husband and citizen, and give him dignity as a worker. The instant the union was formed, the battle began. It would be fought in Queensland. One hundred thousand pounds was collected among the sheep-owners, and within two years all union members were being 'bushed' from properties. Queensland agents went to New Zealand to recruit shiploads of 'free' shearers as well as trainloads from other colonies. The unionists called them 'scabs'.

So the lines were drawn, and it was a grossly unequal struggle. The unionists, locked out of the properties, set up strikers' camps – no easy matter when the new union had no funds to assist its members or their families at home a thousand and more miles away, and the populace was too unversed in such matters to understand their situation. The squatters, having the ear of the government, could call out the police and the army. They also controlled or owned most of the newspapers. Finally, their absolute power put the judiciary in their hands. This last was the hardest pill for the men to swallow.

Men who had come free to the new country, and those born there, could not believe in equality and justice before the law when they were arrested and tried in court by their masters for crimes said to have been committed against these same masters. In time there were real crimes. Wool sheds were burned down, fences cut, animals killed. The infantry, cavalry and artillery were brought into the Queensland outback and under the Irish Coercion Act, which had been rescinded in all British colonies except Queensland, men were arrested and sentenced to hard labour, some for as much as three years.

They were taken in chains and manacles to St Helena island off the coast of Queensland. By now many Australians were in sympathy with them, for the squatters' unjust behaviour had made their own cause suspect. Julian Stuart, the youngest of the men on St Helena, contracted tuberculosis. He wrote: 'One of the warders' wives used to sit outside the window of my cell and read aloud to the empty yard all the strike news and Labor [Party] items. I never saw her face, but often blessed her kindly voice.' The strike lasted for a decade. The shearers lost and returned to work on the sheep-owners' terms, but along with the humiliation they felt some pride. While still in prison the men had heard the news that some Labor members had been elected to Parliament, and Julian Stuart dated the start of his recovery in his prison cell on St Helena as 'the day the Labor men were elected to parliament'. On 1 December 1899 the world's first Labor government sat in Brisbane. It was out of power by the end of the week, but now the men knew that the dream was not impossible.

There were mixed feelings in our family. Grandfather Adams, along with hundreds of other men locked out of the sheds, had walked the thousand miles home. He had sold his packhorse in Queensland, then his hack outside Dubbo

Above: Most of the Shepherd Kings lived in
smart town houses in cities such as Sydney
Opposite: Pitt Street, Sydney, in the late nineteenth
century

in New South Wales. Grandmother, alone with her children in the bush in
Victoria, saw them through Christmas, made dolls for the girls from tree-ferns
and told the boys they were too big now for gifts. 'I didn't like doing it, but
these were lean times,' she told me years later. 'It was sometimes "bread and
point",' referring to the titillating of one's taste buds by stabbing a piece of
bread or potato on one's fork and pointing it at a tiny piece of bacon or an
onion hanging from a hook on the ceiling. For all that, like many independent
country toilers this man was not in favour of either unions or strikes. He only
went along with this one, he said, 'because they were good men and they
weren't being given a fair go'.

During the fiery period of the strike a body of people gathered and declared
that this was indeed no utopia for the working man. They decided to seek
freedom elsewhere and create their own Elysian fields.

> The shearers at Barcaldine had made a mighty stand,
> But the squatters brought the troopers to dominate the land,
> And Lane, the Labor leader, had raised the clarion call,
> 'We'll build a brand new colony where workers will share all!'

Young Mary Cameron – who later, as Dame Mary Gilmore, became one of
Australia's best-loved poets – was going with them.

> O! the men of the new Australia are ready to cross the sea,
> To form a band in a far off land, and show what men they be,
> They are gathering in from the West, and from the Central plain,
> From where the pelican builds her nest and Drought a King doth reign.

William Lane, an impractical theoretician, had decided on distant Paraguay in
South America. The press called it 'one of the most feather-headed expeditions
ever conceived since Sir Galahad pursued the Holy Grail'. The emigrants replied
in verse:

> They say there's Injuns whoopin' round for New Australyin blood,
> Muskeeters big as kangaroos, 'n fever in the mud,
> 'N krockydiles, 'n horrid wars – at least the papers say –
> But there's no Australyin squatters over there in Paraguay.

Men, women and children assembled on the *Royal Tar* on 6 July 1893 to sail
for the hoped-for Promised Land. With them were some of the shearers whose
brave words, deeds and hopes had ended in humiliation and St Helena Gaol.
Among the single migrants was Nurse Clara Jones, who had hoisted a red flag
over Muttaburra hospital in Queensland to celebrate the election of Thomas
Ryan, the first Labor member of the Queensland Legislative Assembly. When

the enraged hospital committee pulled the flag down, Nurse Jones had promptly hauled it up again.

So they sailed off with their charismatic leader, a man who confused socialism with sentiment. He was to lead his people into hardship, loneliness, poverty such as they had never known, and death. Everything they had been warned of came to pass, in a land that had nothing to offer them but a fever-ridden corner of jungle impossible to tame, even by such brave toilers as these. Most of those who had set off with such high hopes scraped together, borrowed or begged enough money to bring them back to Australia, leaving in Paraguay only a handful who would later inter-marry with the tribes native to that area.

This strange, still-born babe of the strikes of the 1880s and 1890s epitomises the canker – or maybe it is the saving grace – of the Australian working class: no man starves to death in this country, even though he may not eat as well as some; no man lacks schooling, although he may not get the education of others; no man goes unclad or quite freezes to death on a winter's night, although he may wear hand-me-downs and pull thin blankets over himself in bed. In short, things are never so bad here as to push him over into revolution against the state, but because the immigrants expected an egalitarian society when they came to the far ends of the earth, their folk-nerve twitched in revolt at the reality.

As for the squatters, their moment of truth was upon them. Before the drought of the 1890s much of western New South Wales carried almost one sheep to every three acres. By 1907, when the effect of overstocking on the fragile native grassland system was revealed, the capacity of most of the properties affected had dropped to one sheep per fifteen acres. Even salt-bush died out in some areas, and no one had thought of that small, grey-green shrub dying. It covers hundreds of square miles in a patch, and grows throughout most of central Australia. Sheep produce good wool on it, but when too many sheep were let loose the fragile balance of nature was broken. The rich western lands of New South Wales were destroyed within twenty years of the arrival of sheep. In 1884, one and a half million sheep grazed on six million acres in the Cobar district. In 1891 twenty-five inches of rain fell there, but still no grass grew: only a green moss covered the land; for nearly twenty years grass refused to grow where it had been killed off. By 1895 the west of New South Wales was a desert, and a loose sand blew until even the fences were covered. Farmers had to try to get their sheep a thousand miles down the eaten-out stock route to the next pasture. Some far-out stations tried to drive their flocks down to Wilcannia and over to Bourke. Most of one mob of ten thousand died on the way, at Louth on the Darling River; only a few hundred survived, 'and these were sold for a few pounds', the *Sydney Morning Herald* reported.

As if there was no end to people's despair, in 1893 the banks crashed. Of twenty-two note-issuing banks, thirteen had closed before the end of the year. Ordinary working people, who for the first time in generations had a little money and had been encouraged to bank it – a penny at a time if they wished – now crowded, angry and afraid, outside the locked doors of the banks. They never saw their hard-won money again. Sheep-owners hung on as long as they could, but what with the strike, the devastating drought and now the banks foreclosing many went to the wall, and many more had their properties taken over by the banks and large companies. 'Marvellous Melbourne', which had boomed since the finding of gold in the 1850s, now went bust, its elegant streets and gracious buildings not to be added to for almost a century. So ended an epoch. Boom or bust, we had seen it all.

At the close of the century the continent of Australia was still a group of colonies, whose young men sailed off to the Boer War with the name of their own colony on their shoulders – they were not yet Australians, but New South Welshmen, Victorians and so on. They saw nothing incongruous about going off to fight fellow-colonials who had battled as hard for their country as they had, and who were being treated as unfairly by Britain as Australia had often been. Some claimed that this participation represented 'Australia entering history', but more than anything else it was larrikinism, that peculiarly Australian term that denotes high spirits and a youthful love of adventure.

Britain had not asked for Australian troops to join in this adventure and was none too pleased when they did arrive and began demonstrating their lack of respect for their 'betters' and utter conviction in their own invincibility. Many of the stories later attributed to the First World War had their origins here on the South African veld – such as the one about an Australian private being arrested and taken before the colonel of the regiment on a charge of refusing to salute officers. 'That's a lie!' the New South Welshman said. 'If they salute me I always salute them back.'

While complaining about their comrades in arms, the British had to admit that their ingenuity and unconventional yet practical approach to discipline were sharper than those of men from the older lands. John Gordon, owner of Ballangeich sheep station in western Victoria, wrote home,

Had a surprise recently. We were sitting on our horses resting, I had one leg across the front of me, when someone yelled, 'There they go!' The Boers! My nag gave such a start my head crashed down and my front teeth were knocked out. I galloped off to the chase with the others but that night I discovered the tragedy: I couldn't eat the army biscuits without teeth!

There was no other food, so he improvised. He put the biscuits in a treacle tin, covered them with water, tied the tin under the horse's neck and galloped off, with the biscuits softening up day after day.

Although they fought some notable battles, the Australians' participation in this war is mostly remembered because of the execution of 'Breaker' Morant.

Harry Harbord Morant, an Englishman, had arrived in Cooktown in the far north of Queensland on 5 June 1883. His family were said to have had gentility, but Harry himself had some rough edges. Cooktown, with its new gold rush, attracted such men, even though the heat, humidity, snakes, malaria and other fevers drove them insane. He worked for a time on a cattle station with horses, from which he derived his nickname, and was a tough man who, like many in his day, could pen a rough bush verse. Morant was typical of many who took their horses across the Indian Ocean to the 'stoush', as they called a fight.

Nothing about him would have given him a place in any country's history if it had not been that, between 27 and 29 August 1901, a fellow-Australian, Lieutenant Peter Hancock had, with Morant's collusion, shot a Boer clergyman, the Reverend C. A. Daniel Hesse, through the chest. The anti-British Hesse had attempted to undermine the loyalty and determination of troops travelling with Morant and Hancock. Until this date British senior officers had not only turned a blind eye to such sporadic killings, but had actually encouraged them. But the British newspapers had reported these atrocities and orders had now arrived that, to avoid an outcry, these acts must be stopped immediately. British policy not to kill unarmed civilians now had to be proved by example: the two Australians were tried by a British court-martial, found guilty and executed. Morant refused a blindfold; his last words to the British firing squad were: 'Shoot straight, you bastards!' Those words remain graven in Australian legend as firmly as do those spoken by Ned Kelly before his death twenty years earlier. Morant's comrades and the Australian public were outraged that their compatriots could be brought before a British court-martial and be executed as a result. The right to bring an Australian to trial, and either free him or decide on his punishment, belonged to his own countrymen, they informed the British in the strongest terms.

At about the same time that this infamous court-martial was being played out across the sea, royalty arrived in Australia to signal their approval to the six colonies achieving statehood within a federation known overall as Australia. Had the horseman galloping around after the Boers with a treacle tin tied round his horse's neck wished it, he could now replace his colonial shoulder flash with the title 'Australia', as would all who left those shores in the future.

The Duke and Duchess of York (later King George V and Queen Mary) were treated to grand parades and passed through flower and fern arches to the Exhibition building in Melbourne. The new federal government would sit in the elegant Victorian Parliament building, while the Parliament of Victoria would trundle round the corner and sit in the big and draughty Exhibition building – until 1927, when the federal Parliament opened in Canberra, which itself was to spring motherless and fatherless into being for that occasion.

But all the shenanigans of floral arches and dukes and feathered hats couldn't hide the facts: federation was entered into unwillingly by some states despite the fact that others saw benefits – even if cupidity rather than noble sentiments

motivated them. Customs and excise between state borders would be abolished and several other matters made uniform, but these new members of a new confederation had been independent colonies far too long to wear a wedding ring easily. They still would have their own Parliaments, each with an upper and lower house; each would have a governor and a judiciary with a chief justice, and retain its own laws, many of them differing from those of their neighbouring states. Each had – and has – its own extradition laws. In fact each state then and now rules itself as if it were a country apart, except for those laws handed down from federal government (if they are sure a state won't revolt against it, or until they can coerce the federal members from such a state to vote for such a bill).

The state that held out the longest was Western Australia. Cut off from the rest of the continent by deserts and arid lands reaching for one thousand miles, this state, which could swallow many European countries within its borders, felt it was as likely to benefit from union with Britain as with the rest of Australia. Intermittently ever since it has threatened secession. The carrot that coaxed this vast and varied colony into federation was the promise of a railway through South Australia to join it with the eastern states. Until then all access had been by sea across the Great Australian Bight, an experience similar to crossing the Bay of Biscay in a storm – only much further. A handful of courageous explorers had crossed by land; the bones of some remain in its moving sands. 'There is no country in the world that has so tried the endurance and perseverance of exploring expeditions as South Australia has done,' wrote a newspaper of this state, which, for its size of population, has the least arable land and the highest proportion of desert and arid land.

The Trans-Australia Railway would join the outposts of Western and South Australia: Kalgoorlie, the centre of gold finds that far outweighed any found elsewhere in the continent, and Port Augusta, a sandy staging-post north of Adelaide. It would be built for over one thousand miles across land that had no running water, no trees to provide timber for construction, and no settlements where labour, provisions or accommodation could be had for the 3500 workmen and the 500 horses and 250 camels that carted for them and broke the ground.

From the beginning the building of the railway depended on camels, the 'desert schooner' that for over a century was the only means of transport for two-thirds of the continent of Australia. From Kalgoorlie survey parties set out with ninety-one camels, blazing their trail with a heavy chain dragged by another group of camels. Surveyors set off at the same time from Port Augusta with eighty camels, and in ten months met up with those coming from the west. The preliminary survey covered 1063 miles. The central area where the two parties joined up now houses the longest straight stretch of railway line in the world. Its 297 miles are so boring for the drivers that they shout 'Whoopee!' if they have to shunt to the curve of a siding at the end.

Along with federation came the Immigration Restriction Bill, later dubbed the White Australia Policy. To a man the Labor Party was for keeping any but 'whites' out. Billy Hughes, later to become Prime Minister, addressed Par- liament during the debate on the bill. 'Coloured people must be rejected because of their immorality, vice, and a hundred things that can only be hinted at,' he said. On 30 March 1901 *The Worker*, Labor's own newspaper, wrote,

A horde of Afghans, Chows and Kanakas coming into this country, insulting your wives and daughters....

What about the coloured alien,
The Chow and the Hindoo?
Men of White Australia
What do you intend to do?

Working men and their political party would later be blamed for the virulence of the Keep Australia White campaign. The Tories' hands were clean because they said 'Bring them in.' But the truth was that they were cheap labour and with luck would bring the white unions into line.

The effects of this bill lasted until after the Second World War. In reality it was no different from, or worse than, the stance of most countries with a white majority, but with the Australian tradition of calling a spade a spade we named the Act to frame its content (or, to quote Arthur Calwell, the architect of our post-1945 immigration policy, 'Two Wongs don't make a white'). The old question was always brought up: 'Would you desire that your sisters or brothers should be married into any of these races?', but the industrial aspect was the more important. Coloured 'undesirables', as Chris Watson, a Labor Member of Parliament, called them, could be tolerated in so far as they took the place of labourers who might be unreliable or not quite so cheap. 'But', said the Hon. Mr Watson,

when it was found that these orientals possessed all the cunning and acumen necessary to fit them for conducting business affairs and that their cheapness of living was carried into business matters as well as into ordinary laboring work, a marked alteration of opinion took place among business men.

The Hon. Billy Hughes said, 'A free people must fear the destruction of their living standards that would come with cheap coloured labour.'

There were several places where, by tacit consent, the Act did not apply. The famous pearling town of Broome depended on island and Japanese divers because the work was not attractive to Europeans. The reason for this lack of attraction is symbolised by the graveyard where hundreds of Japanese lie in graves beneath pastel slabs of rock brought from the nearby coast. Kanakas

Above: 'In 1914 we rushed to the Great War. . . .' A mother and her son make their farewells at Sydney

'The bugles of England were blowing o'er the sea. . . .' A patriotically bedecked recruiting train at Wallumbulla, Queensland

were imported from the Pacific islands to work in the Queensland sugar-cane fields, and their descendants form a community there to this day. Chinese had come out during the gold rushes of the 1850s. And in 1890 Darwin, capital of the Northern Territory, imported three hundred indentured Chinese to build a railway three hundred miles to the south to bring out ore from the mines. These industrious men, to quote an old white railway man, 'were brought out to work for us, [but] had us on their books by the end of their first year here'. They opened shops and cafés, imported foods, and set up tailoring shops, gambling dens and opium parlours. In Australia's bicentennial year Alec Fong Lim, a descendant of one of these indentured railway navvies, is lord mayor of the city.

Federation was said to have been a symbol of unity for the young country, but nations are born out of more pain than this. In 1914 we rushed to the Great War as though the old barbaric tradition of blood sacrifice was demanded of our new nation – and because of old ties. As a student at Scots College, Melbourne, wrote:

> *The bugles of England were blowing o'er the sea,*
> *As they had called a thousand years, calling now to me,*
> *They woke me from dreaming*
> *In the dawning of the day.*
> *The bugles of England*
> *And how could I stay.*

They thought they would be going to France, to the battlefields of the Western Front. But in the few months it took the steamships to bring them twelve thousand miles across the sea the war had already bogged itself down in stalemate. Winston Churchill, then First Lord of the Admiralty and eager for a new initiative, conceived the idea of a second front. He would attack Turkey, who had sided with Germany. This was to be done by a seaborne landing on the Gallipoli peninsula and the taking of the Dardanelles, the vital sea-link to Britain's hard-pressed ally, Russia. It was highly convenient for this plan that the raw and still untried Australian troops were now able to be diverted to nearby Egypt. They would form part of a two-pronged attack: the British and French would land on one part of the peninsula; the Australians, with their near neighbours the New Zealanders – together now called ANZACs (Australian and New Zealand Army Corps) – on another. It was a bold plan, disastrously executed, played out in the arena where the mythical heroes of ancient Greece had stood, immovable until death, at the whim of the gods of war whose footsteps still echo above this place.

A large armada of ships set off, the decks jammed tight with young men, excited, tense, joking. A clergyman was giving the troops a blessing, but his words couldn't be heard over the noise of emery wheels and the sharpening of bayonets. And then, without any drama at all, the word came: 'All right, chaps. No talking now. Cigarettes out.' The next order was: 'Over the side' – into the rowing boats that were waiting to drift them ashore. As the boats left the side of the British ships a whisper ran the whole way along the deck where the British sailors were lined up – 'Good luck, Aussies. Good luck!' And so they drifted inshore. As they got there, they jumped off and ran through the water. Then suddenly they began calling to one another: 'My God, it's the wrong place. They've landed us on the wrong place!' Just then the first shots rang out. They discovered they were pinned at the foot of steep hills with the sea behind them.

Every man was a hero – seven won VCs in one afternoon alone. But the single best-known hero of Gallipoli was Simpson, a stretcher-bearer who carried the wounded down to the beach on the back of a donkey. Until the day the ANZACs landed on Gallipoli stretcher-bearers were not considered proper soldiers by the fighting men. From this day on they were accepted as the bravest of the brave. Simpson's beat was Shrapnel Gully, the highway to the top trenches, and much of it lay in full view of the enemy.

Scrub has grown up now on Shrapnel Gully to soften the contours. Yet you can still stub your toes on rusted bully-beef cans, and find old bullets; still smell the danger, as you come across holes where men have sheltered when wounded, or perhaps trying to escape death. General Bridges was killed here, and you don't hear of many generals being killed by a bullet. Simpson knew of the dangers. When warned, he merely responded with that well-known Australian phrase: 'My worries.'

This hero, who became an Australian legend, was in fact an Englishman who had been in Australia for only three years. John Kirkpatrick Simpson was a boozer, a brawler, a ship's deserter – and a gentle person. Whenever he could, he sent money home for his mother and for the licence fee for his dog he'd left behind him. Back in Shields, at his home in England, his mother wrote to him:

Dear Son,

   You said in your letter I'd find out where you were when the Australians made a start. Well, my lad, the Australians have done gloriously. They've made England ring with their bravery. Jack, my son, my heart is fairly bursting with sorrow and with pride to think you are among such a lot of brave men. But mind, they've paid dearly for their bravery. I saw the Australian list of casualties this morning, and I'm sorry to say, it's very heavy.

The man with the donkey was already dead, shot through the heart twenty-four days after landing. The valour of this very ordinary man reverberated around Australia. It was just what the top brass needed to boost recruitment –

Above: 'For almost the whole of their two and a half years in France and Belgium the Australians were used as front-line and shock troops.' An Australian military band passing through Bapaume

Left: A First World War legend and symbol of Australian courage in the face of danger: stretcher-bearer Simpson and his donkey

Opposite: '"I saw the Australian list of casualties this morning, and I'm sorry to say it's very heavy,"' wrote Simpson's mother. A barge carrying Gallipoli wounded to the hospital ship Gascon

while anxious mothers waited nightly outside newspaper offices to scan the casualty lists.

From the day of the landing the Turks had pinned down the ANZACs to that narrow strip of land along the beach, and three months later they were still there. On the Turkish side a brilliant young leader had emerged, Mustapha Kemal, later to be called Kemal Atatürk, the creator of modern Turkey. He was more than a match for Sir Ian Hamilton and the other ageing generals, playing their vacillating war games far from the sweat and vicissitudes of battle. It was said that Atatürk was a product of his times; General Hamilton was a product of his class. When it was decided to make a move to break the impasse in August, the British still underestimated the tenacity of the Turks and the tactical skill of their new leader. This time they were going to use the new British army, called Kitchener's army. These young men were as yet untried in battle. They were to be brought to the north of Anzac Cove, to Suvla Bay, a very accessible, low-lying bay. They would be able to bring their ships in there in the daytime and advance across the flat land.

To keep the Turks' attention off the British soldiers' landing, the Australians and New Zealanders were to make a series of diversionary attacks at places known as Lone Pine and the Nek. The British meanwhile were to move forward round the back of the Turks and cut them off; then perhaps an advance could be made towards Constantinople. Unfortunately, once landed the British troops stayed on the beach for three days because their aged general had not given any order for them to advance. By the time the British did advance the Australians were dead – and the Turks were ready for the British. That was truly the end of the fighting. After so much sacrifice, so many dead, we hadn't gained one inch of new ground.

The failure of the offensive brought out into the open the incompetence of the British command. A young Australian journalist, Keith Murdoch, castigated them in a series of brilliant, damning despatches. His main target was General Sir Ian Hamilton, whose aloof response to Murdoch's criticism was: 'No gentleman would have said it – and no gentleman would believe it.' But in the event Hamilton was relieved of his command, and Britain's Secretary for War – Field Marshal Lord Kitchener – himself decided to come to Gallipoli to assess the situation. It was now all too obvious that evacuation was the only option.

If the British generals felt humiliation, the ordinary Australian soldier did not. He had stood, unmoving, against great odds, and in so doing had brought fame to his land. The Australians' valour certainly preceded them to France, where they were now sent. They had thought Gallipoli was hell, but there was no name for the nightmare that was the Western Front. Modern weapons poured down on them a continual bombardment such as had never been seen on earth before. And for almost the whole of their two and a half years in France and Belgium the Australians were used as front-line and shock troops.

An Australian lieutenant wrote:

> We are lousy, stinking, ragged, unshaven, sleepless. My tunic is rotten with other men's blood, and partly splattered with a comrade's brains. You always told me I'd stick it alright, and I have. But I'd give anything to be out of it. All of us would. I've seen strong men, who've been through Gallipoli, sobbing and trembling with ague – men who've never turned a hair before.

In just one battle, Pozières, the Australians lost more men dead than they did in the whole eight months on Gallipoli. But it was not all horror. War is, and ever has been, a great spectator sport, and the Australian Light Horse fighting in the sands of the Middle East made a great spectacle. One action alone – the taking of Beersheba – has been described by leading military historians as one of the most daring of all cavalry charges. As a rule the Light Horse did not go into battle with cavalry swords; rather, they rode to the scene, dismounted, took cover and then fought forward. Beersheba was different. They were desperate both for water for their animals and to cut off the supply to the Turks, who held the ancient town, so they galloped straight on and over the Turks in their trenches. While some went on to secure the wells, the other horsemen dismounted and fought the startled enemy into flight.

It was Gallipoli, though, that remained for the Australians the symbol of their sacrifice – not only for the men, but for their people back home. This small country of fewer than five million settlers had been the only country to send an all-volunteer army to the war. Of the 330,000 men who fought, 68 per cent were casualties, the highest per capita of all the Allied nations. One of the most gracious and generous gestures to honour Australia's gallantry and loss was made by America in 1920 when *The New York Times* announced that the USA had won the Davis Cup. While agreeing that jubilation was merited, they said, 'Never forget that little Australia held the cup more times than any other nation since its inception (5 out of 8), and won it again in 1914, immediately before this terrible war began.' Touchingly, the Americans had not challenged Australia for the Cup at war's end. Now, a year later, the trophy was back on their soil, and their team had easily beaten the Australians. 'But always remember', the paper continued, 'the greatest Australian tennis players, their greatest sportsmen, made their last run for the net at Gallipoli, Pozières, Ypres and Fleurbeaux. We take nothing from our sportsmen by reminding ourselves of this.'

All kinds of Australians had gone to fight – the shearers, stockmen, miners, railway navvies, squatters' sons, cow-cockies and boys straight from school. Some came home, some have graves, and some are merely listed on long stone walls, for their bodies were never found – amongst them my mother's brothers, Jack and Steve Adams, who disappeared at Lone Pine, and her cousins Mick Byrne, Dick Smith and Jackie Pierce, who were at the Nek. All were Catholics of Irish descent. Like many Catholics who volunteered, they were fiercely opposed to conscription.

The man who became their spokesman was the Archbishop of Melbourne, Daniel Mannix. This stately, aesthetic Irish intellectual was pitted against the fiery, histrionic Australian Prime Minister from the Welsh valleys, Billy Hughes. The two Celts clashed when Hughes twice attempted – unsuccessfully – to introduce conscription. Mannix said, 'Australia has already lost too many men for a country with so small a population.' Hughes thought it was an Irish plot! The Archbishop, great showman that he was, turned up on St Patrick's Day flanked by a military guard of honour, all Catholic and all wearing the Empire's highest award for valour, the Victoria Cross. These bitter conscription campaigns were to stir up bigotry such as we had not known since the early days of settlement. But all Australians admired irrepressible 'Little Digger' Billy Hughes when he had the last word at the Versailles Peace Conference. The United States President, Woodrow Wilson, asked Hughes what right so small a nation had to a place at the Conference table. Hughes replied: 'The right of sixty thousand Australian dead!'

But politicians' promises are made to be broken, particularly those made in the exigencies of war. Soldier settlers were the great Australian losers after the First World War. A few won in a ballot for better land taken from the huge properties of squatters, but in the main the gassed, the wounded and the mind-shattered were allotted blocks bypassed by earlier settlers who knew land useless-for-anything-but-nature. To my birthplace, Sunset Country, they came to a salt-pan desert that had never been farmed before and has not been since these men and their exhausted families left it after ten years of terrible toil, disillusion and heartbreak. In one year of those ten a few men coaxed a crop to grow – government promptly cancelled their subsidy.

Today no one is permitted to use this arid land, too fragile to tolerate a spade, let alone a plough or the sharp hooves of sheep or cattle. Tourists drive on a sealed highway past the edge of our Sunset Country, now called the Big Desert, and rarely stop. They think it ugly. But to those who broke their hearts there so long ago it remains, perversely, a place of beauty where you could look across to where the flat land fell off the end of a flat world of long, slow sunsets turning the salt lakes into pink seas and ice-floes, with the odd camel team, backs hung with bags of salt, making their way south to the rail siding. I was too small to remember much of it, but the picnics are fast in my mind: rugs and bags spread under the horse-drawn jinker or buggy; baskets of food; the men and some of the women, including my mother and Mary Woollong, a Kulkyne tribeswoman, going off with their guns to hunt rabbits.

It used to be said of bush people that we lived in 'Woop-Woop'. But we *did* get into a country town occasionally, usually on Christmas Eve. A few of those old towns have now been preserved as so-called 'living museums', but they are so gentrified you'd think it was a film set waiting for the cameras to roll.

Both before and after the First World War Australia's children enjoyed the simple pleasures of life. Right: The store in Numurkah as we saw it on Christmas Eve, 1929 Below: Bondi Beach has always been popular, even before the days of surfers and topless bikinis

There's no dusty road, and they don't tie gum boughs on to the veranda posts for decorations any more.

The advertisements that amuse tourists today were once necessities for us. There can't be an Australian of my age who hasn't had a gravel rash rubbed with eucalyptus oil, or taken a few drops of it on a teaspoon of sugar for a cold. The Christmas gift to buy for Dad was tailor-made cigarettes – a change from roll-your-own. Mum once went so far as to buy herself an overcoat from an advertisement at 2s 6d a week. We told her she looked 'real flash'. And she'd earned it. Most nights she would work for hours unpicking old clothes and remaking them for my sister Mick and me. We thought they looked as good as new. We never envied the rich, their clothes or their cars. We didn't have much money, but in our way we were having a lot of fun.

That was the Roaring Twenties, the days of flappers and flaming youth. We didn't see much roaring wickedness out our way, but we knew they did those things in the city – they'd do anything there! And they'd do anything in America too – but we had a soft spot for America, which was closer to our lifestyle than England was. Their country and western music fitted our habits and sentiments – they sang of distance, loneliness, backwoods humour and liveliness. 'By Jingo, aren't they something!' we said when we first heard American bands on the wireless. Along with progress and improvement, Australia was having fun. We'd soon be living it up all right, we thought. As it turned out, we were soon hanging on like grim death. The heart and the memory always soften and diffuse things in time, and what we all forget was that this was the last time any of us thought of the mythical road to Gundagai being anything but a pathway to despair.

The Great Depression lay on Australia as it did on America. One of the first countries to feel its onslaught, it was also the last to recover from it. By 1928 Australia's export prices had begun collapsing, and by 1931 they had fallen to half their pre-Depression value. As early as 1929 the government was forced to float a £10 million short-term loan in Britain which dragged like a millstone round our fiscal neck as each quarter we begged the bankers in London to renew our credit – and encouraged them not to press for the £32 million which fell due at the same time. In 1930 the new Labor government went cap in hand to ask the British government if we could postpone the interest payment on Australia's war debts. But the Bank of England replied, 'Inform your Government to pay to the last shilling.' We thought we had, or was it only to the last man we had paid? We had one of the highest unemployment rates in the world, with 40 per cent of the workforce – many of them returned servicemen – jobless.

We were better off than many – by now we were a railway family. Dad, with his slight body already ravaged by war, was wielding pick and shovel on the track in temperatures that rose to 111 degrees Fahrenheit ('No kneeling to

Opposite: Yarding the
famous thick-fleeced
Merino sheep in New
South Wales

weed, bend your backs!' and 'Heave! Heave! Uh ah! Uh ah! as you lift the rail with your crowbar').

Once a year our family saw how the other half lived, when the Railway Department gave us an open ticket to go anywhere we liked over the two-week holiday period. We virtually rode the rails for those fourteen days and knew every corner of Victoria, our own state, as well as going on long inter-state journeys.

The city always riveted us. Not that we were afraid of it – on the contrary, my sister and I stalked up and down the long city platforms in pride. 'You must be from the bush!' people would say. 'However could you guess?' we wondered. But if they had not guessed, we would have told them. We had no illusions – we *knew* we were superior to any of the hurrying, frowning, snapping people rushing off to shut themselves away from the sunshine for eight hours every day. 'Guess where we come from?' we'd challenge the information officer. 'Waaia!' we'd say, or 'Nowingi, Katamatite, Bet-Bet, Bong-Bong, Briagalong, Wingeel', or whatever outlandish place we'd camped at recently, and he would say to passers-by, 'Come and meet two young ladies from the bush,' and we would grin with pride. Flinders Street Station in Melbourne may have had the greatest number of passengers in the world passing through it, but – we were from up-country! Today we children would be called disadvantaged – no schooling, no books, our playground a dust bowl or the rail track – but in those days we were called battlers. Dad never gave in to bad times – he'd take us miles on rail trolleys to visit other settlers to play cards or sing or just talk.

With the Depression sitting over the land like a wet, grey army blanket, the city lost its excitement for us. We went to visit a railway friend down on his luck in the city and saw an official throw a handful of tickets in the air: scores of men leaped up and fought among themselves, trying to grab a ticket for food or a single day's work. 'Their dignity's gone,' Mum said when we kids laughed at the spectacle of men grovelling and fighting as the tickets fell to the ground. 'They've ripped the pride out of good men.' Our parents both felt with pain the plight of the once-proud, tough Australian working man, and never let us girls forget it.

Soup queues and handouts were poor compensation for men who'd driven trains across a wilderness, travelled the great shearing routes of the outback, boasted of their strength and endurance and been proud of their day's toil. 'What does "redundant" mean?' a man asked Dad. 'They say there's nothing wrong with my work, but I'm not to turn up on Monday because I'm redundant.' Looking out of the train windows as we rattled through the inner suburbs, staring down into their mean little back yards, Mum once said, 'I wonder what's behind those back doors. Some poor woman, I imagine. God help her.'

We knew it wasn't only the labouring classes who were suffering; professional

Left: Since the first days of free settlement Australia has ridden 'on the sheep's back'. A shearing shed in New South Wales

Top: Aboriginal stockmen mustering horses in the Northern Territory. 'They rode as though they'd always known horses, and the roving life of a stockman suited them.'

Above: Australia is a land of legend. This 1940s' photograph shows an old Aborigine who claims to be the hero of the song 'The Man from Snowy River'

The sugar-cane fields of Queensland have
traditionally employed immigrants for the hard
and back-breaking labour involved
Inset: 'My father was a ganger with pick and
shovel, my mother station-mistress at the isolated
sidings.' The oildrum mailbox on its pole was many
outback families' link with the world beyond

Australian painters found ample inspiration in the landscape and daily life of their rugged land.
Right: The Lost Child, *by the late nineteenth-century artist Frederick McCubbin*
Far right: Tom Roberts, Shearing the Rams

Opposite
Below left: Australian troops fought gallantly in both world wars, where their natural spirit of camaraderie stood them in good stead. This recruiting poster is from the First World War
Below right: 'When a boy from Alabama/Meets a girl from Gundagai/There's a silver lining in the sky.' US troops' better pay and smarter uniforms were all too attractive to some Australian girls during the Second World War

A CALL FROM THE DARDANELLES

"Coo–ee–
Won't YOU
come?"

GULF OF SAROS

SEA OF
MARMORA

ENLIST NOW

men knocked on our door asking for work. Dad was now a ganger and every man wanted a job in his gang. Shopkeepers, businessmen, farmers – all were in distress. In 1930 those still in work were victims of the emergency reduction of the basic wage. It brought my father's pay down to £2 17s 6d a week. 'Oh,' people say today, 'but you could buy much more with that in those days.' You could not. It had been designed as enough for a family to survive on – nothing more. For most of the Depression we lived 'Beyond the black stump', that imaginary line where one is out of reach of succour, out in the space where one has only one's own resources and courage to fall back on.

While things were indeed terrible in the cities, in the country no one found words to describe the poverty and fear of isolation. 'Humping his bluey' – carrying his blanket on his shoulder – a man would set off looking for work. The woman would be left alone with her children, without money, taking in washing if she could get it; and then, as often as not, the man would come home months later, still without money. There was no lady bountiful here, no welfare, no medical benefits, no hand-outs. When my father, crippled in an accident on the line, was unable to work for twelve months, Mum put things up for sale. She thought she'd get a pound, perhaps 25s. I was sent to get the money. The auctioneer gave me 1s 9d. There is nothing you do to yourself in the rest of your life that rubs out the memory of that walk home.

That is my memory of childhood. That, and watching tarpaulins lift on rail trucks and seeing pairs of eyes peering out as the trains rumbled by our lonely outposts: the down-and-outs were 'jumping the rattler', looking for work. In our lonely part of the bush they seemed to us like a lost army wandering in search of a leader.

Gundagai was the national symbolic country town of Australia. It was a household word. It twanged the strings of our communal heart that has always looked longingly to the bush, the never-never, the back-of-beyond. We believed we were all part of it. Like most such symbols the world over, Gundagai was in fact none of the things we led ourselves to think it was. It was what we made it in our need for identity with an inland that is too big, too hostile and yet too seductive for us to live easily with it.

Three songs and a poem made Gundagai what it became to a nation. First there was a doggerel verse about a teamster at Five Mile Creek, a few miles out of the little bush town in New South Wales on the road to Melbourne, where teamsters used to camp with their supply carts and heavy-laden bullock wagons high-towered with bales of wool. Many had crossed the black-soil plains where wagons bogged up to their axles, wheels collapsed, whole cargoes had to be unloaded and reloaded, where bullocks and horses strained and the driver cursed. 'He's got a tongue on him like a bullocky,' they said of these men whose lives were built and cemented with hard work:

Opposite above: An old bush town today. Behind the carefully preserved shabby façade, like 'a film set waiting for the cameras to roll', life goes on with all the benefits of the modern consumer society

Opposite below: Early colonial elegance. Apart from the sunshine these terraced houses could be in an English spa town rather than in Sydney

Opposite: Men at work on the construction of Sydney Harbour Bridge, opened in 1932. In order to get a job in these troubled times, many professed to skills they did not have

Right: ' "What does 'redundant' mean?" a man asked Dad.' Many of the hungry jobless were ex-servicemen

Right: 'The Great Depression lay on Australia as it did on America.' Out-of-work men living out their days in a public park

Above: 'Men ventured into the dead heart of the continent and beyond, across more deserts, to the fur-thermost hostile regions.' Their women went with them, leading harsher lives than many of them had experienced before

Right: '"He's got a tongue on him like a bullocky," they said of these men whose lives were built and cemented with hard work'

As I was coming down Conroy's Gap
I heard a maiden cry,
'There goes Bill the bullocky,
He's bound for Gundagai.
A better poor old ——
Never earnt an honest crust,
A better poor old ——
Never drug a whip through dust.

His team got bogged at the Five Mile Creek,
Bill lashed and swore and cried,
'If Nobby don't get me out of this,
I'll tattoo his —— hide.'

But Nobby strained and broke the yoke,
And poked out the leader's eye,
Then the dog sat on the tucker box
Five miles from Gundagai.

It seems an innocuous enough piece of rough bush verse, but hardly the stuff of which legends are made – until you learn the truth. Now remember this: the bullocky had been through all the vicissitudes of a hard trip; everything that could smite him had smitten him. And what's the punch line that really finishes him off? 'The dog sat on the tucker-box.' A big wooden box in which the food was stored. Why shouldn't the dog sit on it? Everyone else sat on tucker-boxes in the bush. Ah, but the dog didn't *sit* on it. He really blotted his copybook. Probably the excitement made him do it. Anyway, all the tucker had to be tossed out.

It was that strange prudery of the period that published 'sat' instead of 'shat'. Indeed, in the original verse are the two words most used by Australians since Governor Phillip minced up the beach with his convict crew in 1788 and got his feet wet. 'The Dog on the Tucker-Box' was well known in the late nineteenth century and men brought it back south after the shearing strikes of the 1880s and 1890s.

At this time, one of our most popular books was *On Our Selection*, the saga of small farmers – cockies; and like small farmers anywhere they were always down on their luck. The rain always came too early or too late, they were always fighting fires, floods or drought, always being threatened with foreclosure or eviction. In the 1930s a series of films was made of them, featuring Dad the patriarch and Dave the country yahoo, with Mum, Mabel and Joe and other bush characters. Funny and painfully poignant, they swept across Australia in the films and as a serial on the wireless.

Dad and Dave was the most popular serial ever broadcast in Australia; one of

*Right: 'It was a grand background for a life.' A family outing in 1928
Below: My father's family, forced out of Scotland during the Highland Clearances, became timber-men in the forests of Victoria*

Far left: 'We were better off than many – by now we were a railway family'

Left: Today we children would be called disadvantaged – no schooling, no books, our play-ground a dust bowl or the rail track – but in those days we were called battlers'

Below: The little farms in the Gippsland bush where we visited relatives were thought by us to be very 'way back'. We were used to the bustle of a railway station, and let everyone know it

the reasons for its success was its theme song, 'Along the Road to Gundagai'. Jack O'Hagan, a much-loved singer and composer, had written it in the 1920s. He didn't really have 'Gundagai' in mind, at first. 'I thought, wouldn't it sound well to have four syllables, like Mississippi. Then, what about the Murrumbidgee River in New South Wales? Oh, yes, and Gundagai is on that river!' Of such stuff are legends made. We sang the song from one end of Australia to the other. Together with 'My Mabel Waits for Me' and a Second World War song, 'When a Boy from Alabama Meets a Girl from Gundagai', it made an otherwise ordinary country town famous.

We loved *Dad and Dave*. After all, they were just gentle caricatures of us bushwhackers, or 'bushies' as they say today. Our family had the only wireless in the area, and every weeknight people came from miles around by horse, bike, cart and beaten-up tin lizzies to listen in with us. At 7 p.m. we'd hear the music start up – you didn't turn on until then in case the battery went flat: we were twenty miles from the nearest town where we could get it recharged. We'd crowd into the 'front' room, up close to the big speaker, and through the static we'd hear the voices that made us laugh or cry or tremble. *Dad and Dave* did all those things to us. I'll always remember when Dad was about to lose Snake Gully, his farm, in a drought. He came in and said, 'Well, Mum, it's come to this.' I'll never forget Mum's reply: 'Dad, we started from nothing and we'll start from nothing again.' As all of us bush people crowded around, knowing what that meant, the tears poured down our faces.

Laughter and tears were all mixed up together in the Depression. Things that embarrassed the bigwigs were occasions for us to roll around with mirth. Such a day was the opening of the 'coat-hanger', as the wags called the Sydney Harbour bridge, with its great single span one of the engineering feats of the day. It was our pride and joy, and the final joining of the two arches was the focus of the nation. But by the time it was finished it had cost sixteen lives. The unemployed, desperate for work, lied about their inexperience and sweated in fear and terror on the rigging high above the beautiful harbour. The bridge cost nine million Australian pounds and it took the New South Wales government fifty-two years to pay for it.

The opening on 19 March 1932 was much more exciting than such things normally are. I knew this was so, even though I was only eight years old, because I was visiting my Grandma who listened to the broadcast of the ceremony on her cat's whisker crystal wireless and relayed it all to me. Mr Lang, the Labor Premier, was being his usual abrasive self. He was the epicentre of controversy because he had refused to pay the interest due to British stockholders who had invested in New South Wales. He said the state needed the money 'more than those bowler-hatted bastards in London'. The public had wanted royalty brought out to perform the opening ceremony, but Premier Lang declared he would do it himself because it would be cheaper. His attitude had provoked the formation of an extreme right-wing paramilitary group, the

New Guard. Suddenly, as Lang prepared to cut the ribbon, an officer on horseback galloped forward brandishing a shining sword and shouting, 'In the name of common decency I declare this bridge open!' He slashed the ribbon. Major Francis de Groot had beaten Jack Lang to the punch.

Grandma was alarmed but Grandad had just come in and he laughed – not because he agreed with de Groot, but because of the excitement. Anything was welcome to relieve the doldrums of the Depression.

There were even more heroic gestures than de Groot's taking place at the time. Australian airmen were shrinking the map, perhaps because we still felt ourselves to be on the extreme edge of it. With outposts separated from each other by hundreds or even thousands of miles it was natural for Australia to be in the forefront of flight and air travel. As far back as 1878 the aviation pioneer Lawrence Hargrave was respected worldwide for his study of flight; in the early days he concentrated on observing the movements of birds, insects and fishes until he discovered the three movements essential for flight. The rotary engine he invented in 1889 with revolving cylinders attached to propeller blades was the forerunner of that which powered Blériot's monoplane. Men were building aircraft in their back yards – and flying them – by 1910. Well, some flew, and some remained in back yards, but the spirit was there.

After the war broke out in 1914 Australian airmen had some exciting and sometimes dangerous adventures. Tom (later Sir Thomas) White once set off to rescue the chief of staff of Mesopotamia, whose seaplane had been forced down in the desert. Tom landed amid Arab fire, only to find the weight of Major-General Kemball too great for the plane to become airborne. It meant a journey home across the sand, driving the plane like a car. Frank (later Air Vice-Marshal) MacNamara won a VC when, wounded as he landed to try to rescue a downed pilot, he set off under fire with the grounded pilot hanging on to his fuselage. But MacNamara, weak from his wound, was unable to control the plane with the passenger hanging on. So he landed and set fire to his aircraft, then the two ran to the other wrecked plane on the ground, got it going and flew the seventy miles back to base.

Many flew and fought in the air of Egypt, Mesopotamia, France and Belgium, and at war's end decided to keep on flying – home to Australia. They were willing to do it just for the hell of it, but on 1 March 1919 the Commonwealth government offered a prize of £10,000 for the first Australian to fly from England to Australia in an Empire-built aircraft within a period of thirty consecutive days. Four men from No. 1 squadron, Australian Flying Corps won the race – Captains Ross and Keith Smith and Aircraftsmen Wally Shiers and Jim Bennett.

For the twenty-seven days of their flight they piled excitement on top of excitement. To take off from the glue-like mud at Pisa Jim Bennett sat on the tail to effect a lift in the nose skid, which had been digging in the mud. When

Opposite above: 'Australian airmen were shrinking the map, perhaps because we still felt ourselves
to be on the extreme edge of it.' Wherever they
went, they attracted large crowds
Opposite below: 'Australia's heroes came from all
walks of life.' The Narrabeen Life-saving Corps
parading at Manly Beach, Sydney

Above: 'That was the Roaring Twenties, the days
of flappers and flaming youth'

131

the biplane took to the air Jim had to be hauled on board and dragged into the open cockpit. They near-froze and near-boiled; their Vickers Vimy began to blow away in Baghdad until they recruited fifty Iraqi soldiers to lie on top of it. Birds collided with them and treetops threatened to impale them. In Thailand, the so-called airstrip was studded with tree stumps – and flooded. But they made Darwin on 10 December and the entire population, admittedly only a few hundred at that time, turned out to welcome them as they taxied down the main street to take the prize. They were greeted, as they deserved to be, as successors to the explorers of old who had shrunk the map with their camels and bullocks.

Hinkle Hinkle little star
Sixteen days and – here you are!

Actually it was fifteen and a half days that Bert Hinkler took to fly his Avro Avian on the first solo flight from Croydon in England to Darwin in Australia. Hinkler, the ex-Royal Naval airman, had been breaking solo records since the war ended. He flew 1046 kilometres from England to Italy in his Avro Baby, a long-distance record. The following year he bettered his own record by flying 1130 kilometres from Sydney to his home town of Bundaberg in Queensland.

Of all Australian aviators it was 'Smithy', Sir Charles Kingsford Smith, MC, who won the affection of the country. We have sung songs about him, written books about him, made films of his exploits. One of the war's daring young men with helmet and goggles, scarf flowing from the open cockpit, he had come home and gone barnstorming from one dusty bush town to the next to earn funds for attempts at record-breaking.

While Lindbergh flew the Atlantic, we reminded ourselves that Smithy crossed the much wider, less safe Pacific, leaving from Oakland in California and touching down at Brisbane. He created record after record: in a few short years not only were other lands now brought close to us, but all points of Australia were becoming only a few days away from one another. Then in 1929 he flew out of favour, because of what many see as the fickle flaw of Australians: we place haloes around the heads of our chosen heroes, and just as quickly cast the halo and the head down when we grow weary of them being on the pedestal we so carefully erected for them.

Whether Smithy deserved his fall from grace we shall never know. The facts are these: on 31 May 1929, along with three other fliers he set off for England in his plane, the *Southern Cross* – and disappeared for twelve days in the remote Kimberley area of north-west Australia. When found, Kingsford Smith said he and his crew had been forced down for repairs. In the meantime a search party had set out across the arid wastes to look for the man who was everyone's ideal: two of its members had died in the attempt. Overnight Smithy was a villain. It was suggested he needed money – but airmen always did – and had faked

his disappearance to gain publicity for his new attempt on the record. Although
he set off again immediately and did set a new record for the Australia–England
flight, and continued for seven years to add to his impressive lists of achievements
for Australia, he was never again hoisted on the pinnacle of fame where we
ourselves had placed him.

Australia was producing heroes from all walks of life, as if to remind the
Mother Country that we were children no longer. We played *their* game,
cricket, as if we'd invented it, and in 1930 produced 'The Don', Don Bradman,
a cricketer so effective that within three years of his entering international
cricket the English Test team were ordered to stop him. To us, Jardine was just
the kind of English captain who would have sparked off the great bodyline
controversy; even his clipped, Pommie voice rankled us when we heard it on
the wireless.

It was 1933. My father had brought me down to 'the big smoke'. I was going
to watch my first Test match. When Jardine ordered his fast bowler, Harold
Larwood, to aim for the body, Australians fell like men on the battlefield and
all hell broke loose. Everyone jumped up, shouted, leaping over the wooden
benches and making threats. All except my Dad, the quiet bushman. He sat
quietly and I could scarcely hear his voice amid the uproar as he told me, 'They
shouldn't have done that.' I then *knew* it was *wrong*. The next day the newspapers
suggested we should consider seceding from England. That's the depth of
feeling we had about cricket.

It was the best of times and the worst of times. In the midst of the misery
there was excitement, and often events to boost our pride. Australia was trying
to get itself going again after the loss of our youngest and best in the First
World War. The Duke of York and his Duchess (whom we know nowadays
as the Queen Mother) had come out in 1927 to open Parliament at our new
federal capital, Canberra, built out in the bush on the site of an old sheep station.
After the Duke's speech, the woman Europe had declared as having the greatest
voice ever known, Dame Nellie Melba, sang the National Anthem. In opera
there has never been another like her.

When Melba died, on 23 February 1931, it is said that her last words were a
few bars of 'Ave Maria'. And so, in Sir Landon Ronald's words, 'the most
glorious voice God ever put into the throat of a woman' fell silent. She was
said by critics to have had great personal faults, but to us she was a true-blue
Australian who had brought us glory. Up in the bush we had heard her sing
on the gramophone but never seen her. None the less we were as poignantly
distressed at her passing as the few in the cities who had seen and heard her. All
Australia mourned this great woman whose career had spanned almost forty
years. At the age of sixty-four she sang at Covent Garden, and her 'Addio'
from *La Bohème* on that occasion had been recorded. 'The day of the great
coloratura soprano has gone,' said Sir Landon Ronald during a requiem broadcast on the BBC. Melba had died in Sydney, but had wanted to be buried in

Right: Women as well as men enjoyed sports. These three young Sydney ladies are enjoying an interlude in a game called vigoro

Right: 'We played their game, cricket, as if we'd invented it.' Don Bradman (right) and Woodfull (left), stride out to open an innings during the Australians' British tour in 1934

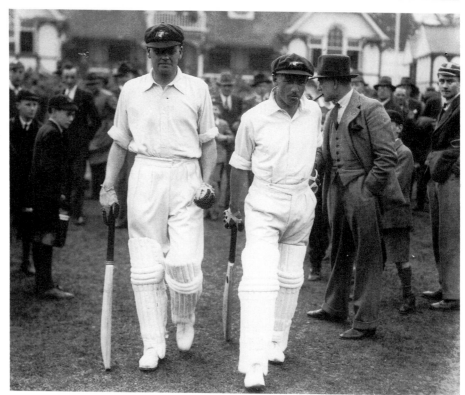

her home town of Lilydale, near Melbourne, to which her coffin was borne by special train. She had returned triumphant on this railway in 1902 at the height of her brilliant career, when the crowds had shouted, sung, waved and thrown flowers in adulation. Now they were silent, many of them weeping.

Before I came to the city I used to cut out newspaper pictures of opera stars and paste them on the thin walls of our house up-country. I was a grown woman before I ever saw an opera, but like many others I often wondered how Australia came to produce so many great singers – particularly women. It's certainly not because we enunciate clearly – some people say we don't even open our mouths when we speak in case the flies get in! Whatever the cause, some beautiful voices did develop here. The consummate purity of the notes that came from Melba's throat mesmerised audiences – and won her the patronage of kings (to say nothing of the scandal-making attentions of certain noblemen). I never saw her, but I did see Marjorie Lawrence. A fine horse-woman, she's the only singer I know to have leaped on a horse and galloped full-pelt on to the stage as Brünnhilde – then sing with the voice of an avenging angel. As for Joan Hammond, few singers could claim her absolute control and immaculate phrasing; her 'O, my beloved father' is perhaps the greatest record-ing ever made of that particular aria. And then there's *La Stupenda*, as the Italians call Joan Sutherland. Like Marjorie Lawrence she retained her own special, unspoiled Australian persona even when she had the operatic world at her feet.

The source of much of this rich artistic life was an aspect of Australian life that is often seen only in negative terms. The squatters (or pastoralists as they nowadays like to be called) have often been damned, but it should not be forgotten that the wealth they produced not only feathered their own nests but by the first decade of the twentieth century had made Australia the world's wealthiest nation per capita. Both musicians and other artists contributed to the surge of artistic wealth that matched the material wealth from off the sheep's back.

It is often said that we Australians remember the worst of our past; we ignore the best. Our films of the 1970s and 1980s were heralded as though we had just discovered celluloid, yet in fact we were involved in film-making at a very early stage. With our reputation for gambling it is not surprising that the first 'film' shot in Australia was of scenes at the Melbourne Cup in 1896. By 1904 spectators were able to see martyrs beheaded, crucified, hacked to pieces and fed to the lions in *Soldiers of the Cross*. It had cost £600, was shot on a tennis court at a home for girls, and produced by the Salvation Army's cinematographic unit. *The Story of the Kelly Gang*, using three miles of film, was screened in 1906 and claimed to be the first feature-length film. (*The Great American Train Robbery*, made in 1903, ran for twenty minutes and used only eight hundred feet of film; it is usually considered too short to be regarded as a feature film.) The bushranger Ned Kelly, with his fellow outlaws Dan Kelly, Steve Hart and Joe Byrne, rode across the screen less than thirty years after

Above: Dame Nellie Melba, 'the woman
Europe had declared as having the greatest
voice ever known'. When she died some four
years after this picture was taken all Australia
mourned her passing
Right: Opera singer Joan Hammond enter-
taining troops in 1939

they'd been gunned down in their real-life shoot-out. It mightn't have been art and it didn't have the technique of an Ingmar Bergman, but it was a feature film as good as any being produced at the time and it does show how skill – and legends – can establish themselves in Australia as quickly as in the American Wild West.

At about the same period Australian painters began to be less influenced by European artists. They painted native trees with their bark peeling off instead of autumn leaves falling, depicting the landscape of their native land with all the characteristics that make the expatriate Australian long for home.

Among the Australian legends that have always fascinated us are the stories of those men who set off on immense, mad endeavours, as though 'life were but a little thing worth the gambling. . . . ' The psychological effect of having this vast, empty frontier is great; America no longer has it. Men ventured into the dead heart of the continent and beyond, across more deserts, to the furthermost hostile regions such as the north-west part of the continent, Kimberley – a region so vast that the British Isles and Scandinavia would be lost in it. Here everything is larger than life. Though a man's land ownership is limited by law to one million acres, some owners 'dummied' and built up cattle stations of six to eight million acres.

Overlanders drove cattle from as far as three thousand miles away to stock Kimberley, and our stockmen were heroes long before Hollywood mythologised the cowboy. In a land without fences a stockman would be out months at a time mustering – rounding up cattle to be branded or driven to ports on their way to market. Strings of pack donkeys with bells tinkling round their necks carried the cooking gear; a horse 'tailer' hobbled the hundred or so horse 'plant' – in the hot, humid weather a man might need three horses a day; and at nightfall, his head on his saddle, he slept under the stars. Each cattle station was self-sufficient, the size of a small country town, making its own entertainment.

When I first went up to Kimberley forty years ago, I thought cattle were one of the few things the early pioneers brought to Australia that didn't rob the Aborigines of all their dignity – even though property owners did rob them of a decent wage. They rode as though they'd always known horses, and the roving life of a stockman suited them. Proud of their skill, they flaunted ten-gallon hats and flashy shirts as symbols of their status.

While the traditional life of the Aborigine may have been over-idealised, there's no doubt that the two hundred-year encounter between white and black has been catastrophic. Today it has become fashionable to damn missionaries for this, but they were the only organised body who acted as a buffer between a pioneer, expansionist society and a people who, because they had been isolated on this large island for a hundred thousand years, were defenceless. During my childhood, missionaries trained girls beautifully – to be house servants. But outside the stern discipline and protective walls of the mission much worse

could happen. Absentee landlords such as Lord Vestey kept them in slave conditions. Even in my time, in 1937, seven black girls helped build a hundred-mile road to Vestey's Wave Hill Station in the Northern Territory. Their overseer, Matthew Thomas, wrote that they worked longer and harder than the men, with pick, shovel and crowbar. They used flour bags to cover their naked bodies and were paid with tobacco, beef, tea and sugar.

In 1938 the writer Bill Harney married a girl he'd first seen harnessed to a plough with twenty other black women. There was many a fine relationship – even marriages – between white men and black women, in spite of co-habitation between races being illegal until 1967. And when children came along, especially if they were conspicuously light-skinned, the authorities' reaction was to rescue them from what was termed 'the blacks' camp'. Hilda Muir, now a proud grandmother, was one of them. She was taken from the blacks' camp at Borroloola and brought to Darwin to be educated and trained as a nurse. Part of the so-called Assimilation Policy introduced in the 1920s, it meant that Hilda Muir never saw her mother again – when, forty years later, she went back to her birthplace, her mother was dead. Hilda became a nurse and married a ship's engineer. In the climate of the times this was like an escape.

Some saw the Aborigines in those days as outcasts, on a par with the Chinese. Others said they were a doomed people, and all that could be done for them was 'to smooth the dying pillow', in the words of Daisy Bates, a pioneer worker among the tribes. In the isolated regions we lived in we always knew blacks, and my parents and we kids always had black friends, so I didn't see it that way. My friend Dollery and I planned to go and find work together some day.

We didn't know the Depression had ended until the war began in September 1939. And then Bob, my twenty-two-year-old brother-in-law, said 'It's a job, anyway.' His expression was one of relief, a release from the times he had grown up in.

We were then living in a little country town and all the young boys vanished, many of them 'jumping the rattler' down to the city to their first job. It is said that a large proportion of the 6th Australian Division was formed of veterans of the Depression. Troop convoys formed up at the major ports and set off to battlefields in places far away. Women wept, partly in fear but partly from the vista of loneliness and boredom they could see stretching ahead down here at the bottom of the world, as far as one possibly could be from the scene of action and excitement. That's how it had been for the women in the last war, hadn't it?

In some ways events moved swiftly. Germany invaded Poland on 1 September; on 3 September Britain and France declared war on Germany, as did Australia and New Zealand. Our 6th Division left home in December 1939 and sailed for the Middle East on 11 January 1940, followed by the 7th to Syria

Opposite: Between the Depression and the war we found a little time to enjoy ourselves A motor party driving through the bush near Alice Springs (above), and a group of debutantes and their partners at a parish ball in 1939 (below) I am on the far left of the middle row

and, later, the 9th to go with Montgomery across North Africa. 'The Empire is now alone!' was the cry on hearing of the capitulation of France on 22 June 1940. Some of our men were already in Britain, but none of our servicemen was in action until 19 July when HMAS *Sydney* sank the Italian cruiser *Bartolommeo Colleoni*, our first sea battle in that war.

In the Middle East Australians were to die fighting for Bardia, Benghazi and the much lauded victory at El Alamein, but already before the end of April 1941 we knew the thrill of Tobruk – non-combatants twelve thousand miles away must have something to urge them on to keep the money and sons rolling in to the coffers of war. This rocky, isolated desert outpost was under siege – 'a state of siege', that most ancient term of warfare, thrilled the nation. Our men held it against all the time-honoured siege weapons: lack of food, fuel, drinking water, ammunition and relief. British ships and the five aged Australian naval ships crept in under cover of the darkest nights to bring supplies and take off the wounded.

A renegade Englishman, known as 'Lord Haw-Haw', broadcast from Berlin. 'You are like rats living in holes in the ground,' he told the Australian soldiers. 'We're the Rats of Tobruk!' they shouted in glee – and they retain the name to this day. He called the little rusty old Australian ships 'The Scrap Iron Flotilla', and this *nom de guerre* too was seized with pride.

When HMAS *Sydney* came home, steaming through the Heads on 11 February 1941, our pride tumbled out in a tumultuous welcome. Two hundred thousand lined the streets as the sailors marched from Circular Quay to Sydney Town Hall for lunch. We shouted, waved and threw kisses as Captain Collins swung into view leading his men in a victory march. Dressed in summer whites they were young, beautiful and proud. No girl, no mother, watching them swing past would believe, had she been told, that every one of them would be dead in nine months' time. Helen Power wrote:

> *Would my heart tell me if you came to die,*
> *And I should see your spirit winging by*
> *A swift white bird against grey sea and sky?*
> *Ah! love, be sure my inmost soul would guess,*
> *Warned by the stirring of a strange distress,*
> *The meaning of its sudden loneliness.*

But, in the meantime, there was plenty for them to do in Sydney and Melbourne. The lights were still on in Sydney, and Bette Davis and Charles Boyer were starring in *All This and Heaven Too*.

On 18 February troops of the 8th Division with their oval colour patches landed in a lush, tropical land closer to home – Singapore. 'Impregnable Singapore', we called it. A true bastion of Empire, its great guns bristled out facing the sea, a warning to all who meddled with the Empire. All this seemed a little more like war to patriotic Australians, isolated with New Zealand in the southern hemisphere.

By 11 April Australians were fighting in Greece; but by the 27th the Germans had entered Athens, and within three days all the British and Australian troops had been withdrawn to the island of Crete. We had scarcely found Crete on our maps when, on 20 May, the German paratroopers began their attack on the island and overwhelmed the defenders. On 2 June we were told that the position on Crete was 'desperate'. Then: 'Half Crete army saved!' – 'But on which half is my Raymond?' my Aunt Maggie cried.

'Crete evacuation an epic!' the papers heralded. 'The entire evacuation was an almost incredible epic that gave the world a new record of courage and daring.' HMAS *Perth* had taken thirteen hundred men from Crete. 'They did not see a single British plane for days.' But they had seen six hundred German planes as well as transports landing paratroopers and infantry. 'After she left Crete with the men she rescued, *Perth* was bombed solidly for seven hours one day and thirteen the next.'

The difficult thing for those waiting at home was that the news releases were so shamefully gung-ho, and so wickedly censored, that the reader could neither believe them nor sift the truth from the propaganda. But they did know some things: it was bad, and the Australians had been hit hard, and indeed it would be true that the gallant HMAS *Perth* had been plastered for as long as the news item said it had. 'No official estimate of killed or wounded, or of those taken prisoner, has been issued,' said the press. Long, long after, the truth came out: 3102 Australians had been taken prisoner by the Germans, and there had been 781 casualties.

We took little heed of the Japanese landing in Indo-China on 27 July. We said we didn't trust that country, Japan. We knew of their brilliant defeat of the Russian navy at Port Arthur in 1904, the first time a 'yellow' race had defeated a 'white' race. And we knew of their cruel rampage through China but ... no, it did not thread fear through our veins at all. Japanese cameras were still music hall jokes, as were their bandy legs, bloodthirsty manner of ritual suicide, short-sightedness and 'inability to walk because their legs are not strong, owing to babies being carried too long on their mothers' backs'. However, even we sent troops to 'the Far East' – which to us is the near north – dressed in good Australian woollen khaki. They went to Malaya, Java, Sumatra and a half dozen unimportant little islands whose names we then scarcely knew, and indeed were not sure of until war's end when the truth was told of the deaths of one in three of our men held captive there.

Our own time was now nearing and, as if to prepare us, in November the great HMS *Ark Royal* was torpedoed and sunk. Five days later, on 19 November, HMAS *Sydney* was sunk 'with total loss of personnel'. Dear God, we prayed, not those boys we had cheered as they marched through Sydney so few months ago? Not *all* those lovely boys? Not our cousin Bertie,

*Above: 'It's a job, anyway.' For many unemployed
Australians the outbreak of war in 1939 was
greeted with relief. Troops waiting to sail for the
Middle East*

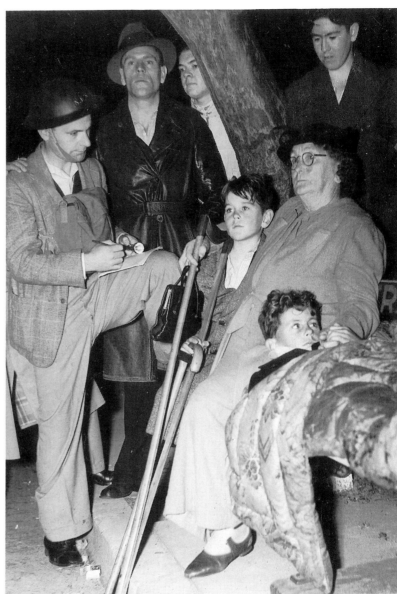

Above: Civilians, evacuated from their homes during the shelling of Sydney by a Japanese submarine, are attended to by a warden

not those golden boys who winked at us girls as they marched up the steps of Sydney Town Hall? Not that boy Nugent we went to school with at Warragul? But yes, they were gone; the sea had devoured their ship and we saw them no more. We had three weeks left in which to mourn. Then Japan attacked the American fleet at Hawaii and declared war on Britain and the USA.

Now it all moved too fast for us to follow without fear. It moved too inevitably, too disastrously. Islands were over-run and our men who defended them disappeared. The day after Australia entered the war against Japan, Nauru and Ocean Islands were attacked, as were Singapore and the Gilbert Islands, and Japan had begun its offensive in northern Malaya. The following day, 10 December, HMS *Prince of Wales* and HMS *Repulse* were sunk off the coast of Malaya. Guam, the Philippines, Hong Kong, North Borneo, Sarawak, Papua, New Guinea, Penang, Rangoon, Wake Island – all were under attack; more than half were administered by Britain or Australia. That Christmas Day the Japanese took Hong Kong, and by New Year they were advancing steadily down the Malayan peninsula.

The first bombs to fall on Australian (mandated) territory (as opposed to British territories north of our coastline) fell on Rabaul, where our young 2/22nd Battalion was awaiting attack. The Americans were pushed from Manila to the island of Corregidor; Kuala Lumpur, Dutch Borneo and the Celebes had fallen; one hundred aircraft carried out the second raid on Rabaul, on 20 January 1942. The next day, in Papua and New Guinea, Lae, Salamaua, Bulolo, Madang and New Ireland were all bombed, as was Manus Island. We made no new ground; we just kept losing it. On the 22nd a Japanese invasion fleet was seen approaching Rabaul and the civilians were evacuated into the jungle, as the 2/22nd Battalion manned their machine gun posts on the beach at Blanche Bay and waited.

We heard no more of that battalion for some time; they managed to hold out for twenty-four hours, we later learned, and then the remnants took to the jungle and waited their chance to escape from the island. On the 23rd the Japanese occupied Rabaul, and by the last day of that month the British and Australian forces had been pushed off the Malayan peninsula to Singapore Island. On Ambon, a small island north of Darwin, the 2/21st Battalion had met the invasion fleet and now they, like the 2/22nd, were lost to us. We heard nothing more of their fate for three and a half years.

And so it continued. Singapore fell on 15 February and Darwin in mainland Australia was bombed on the 19th, killing 246 people. Darwin shocked us, but impregnable Singapore had shaken us to the core. Twenty-two thousand Australian men and nurses were taken prisoner, a devastating number given our population of only seven million. Those of us who were here at that time experienced a surge of emotion that only Mary Gilmore, our best-known patriot-poet, could articulate for us:

We swear by our dead, and captive sons —
Revenge for Singapore!

She spoke for us all in 'Nationality':

I have grown past hate and bitterness,
I see the world as one;
Yet, though I can no longer hate,
My son is still my son.

All men at God's round table sit
And all men must be fed;
But this loaf in my hand,
This loaf is my son's bread.

And, in the dramatic 'No Foe Shall Gather Our Harvest', she expressed our fierce pride at being one with our country:

Our women shall walk in honour,
Our children shall know no chain,
This land that is ours forever
The invader shall strike at in vain.
Anzac! ... Bapaume! ... and the Marne!
Could ever the old blood fail?
No foe shall gather our harvest,
Or sit on our stockyard rail.

We are the sons of Australia,
Of the men who fashioned the land,
We are the sons of the women
Who walked with them, hand in hand;
And we swear by the dead who bore us,
By the heroes who blazed the trail,
No foe shall gather our harvest,
Or sit on our stockyard rail.

We did not know until war's end of the great loss of life in the raids upon Darwin, and of course we didn't know the truth of Singapore or Ambon, but those two islands had held the darling boys of many an Australian home, as had Rabaul and other islands where the 8th Division had been scattered. There was no respite, scarcely time to register one shock, before another struck. On 14 March the Prime Minister, John Curtin, announced:

AUSTRALIA   Information has been received from the Naval Board that HMAS *Perth* and HMAS *Yarra* are overdue on their return to Australia from waters around Java. In view of the circumstances surrounding operations in that area it is with deep regret that I announce that these two ships must be presumed lost. An enemy claim to this effect was made some days ago. There has been no news of survivors.

Brave, brave *Perth* that had survived twenty-one bombing attacks in her bid to rescue the living from Crete. Brave, drowned boys. Again, Mary Gilmore voiced our feelings:

> *We are the women who mourn our dead.*
> *Yea. Let us weep for them.*

It was the season for tears, and each day brought dark news. General MacArthur had left his men on Bataan and Corregidor and was now in Melbourne. His melodramatic 'I shall return' utterance, made at a bush landing strip south of Darwin, became an American legend and an Australian catch-phrase. A diner in a Melbourne restaurant is said to have overheard the following:

> *Diner:*   Can you serve us now?
> *Waitress:*   I shall return.
> *Diner:*   Thank you, Mrs MacArthur.

The press repeated MacArthur's every word with reverence, even to the effect that he was 'surprised and disappointed' to find no army in Australia. Hell, we said, doesn't he know that although America has only been in the war for three months, we have been fighting for two years and six months, and our fighting men have been the other side of the world for most of that time? Our Prime Minister would now order them home – to the unforgiving anger of Winston Churchill who claimed that Britain's need was greater and that, after Germany had been defeated, a defeated Australia could be freed. But the enemy was now at *our* gate and this time it was *our* survival that was at stake. Our response to Churchill could be summed up in 'When', by Phillip Lyons.

> *When our last ship's been torpedoed,*
> *And our last plane drops in flames,*
> *When our one last friend has ditched us*
> *And we're lonely in our shame –*
> *When deserted, bankrupt, weakened,*
> *We're exhausted, tired and blue,*
> *Then we'll have to take the white flag out*
> *And tell the world we're through.*

When bereft of our resources,
We are robbed of all our strength,
When we pray for one last fighting chance
Before we sink at length,
And it's denied us when we're ready
To hoist the white flag high —
Hold on! there's still one better thing,
And we'll do it first — we'll die!

In 1942 Jack O'Hagan wrote:

When a boy from Alabama
Meets a girl from Gundagai
There's a silver lining in the sky.

Now America was in the war. Of course Australians repeated many of the sorts of things said in the First World War: 'Where were they in 1939?' – 'They didn't worry about Hitler, did they?' – 'Waited to be dragged in.' Old soldiers said, 'At least they've seen water!' To the shower-conscious Australians – some believe showering is a fetish among us – the memory of the British in the First World War was still vivid. 'If you want to frighten a Pom,' they said, 'show him a dish of water!'

It was of course mutual help: America needed a base in the south-west Pacific and we, along with New Zealand, were the friendly nations down in the watery end of the world. Prime Minister Curtin had confirmed what we already knew – that Britain could no longer aid or protect us. So for the first time in its history Australia had the reassurance of a great ally on its own soil. The presence of hundreds of thousands of Americans in our time of peril should have been a constant delight to us. Instead, almost from the outset it was a festering sore.

The USA was committed to the defence of Australia, which should have been enough to assure their servicemen of welcome, but mankind does not respond in such simple, uncomplicated ways. We had not seen our own fighting men since they sailed away to war in 1939. Many were now dead; many more were reported missing, existing in the limbo land of women's minds – over thirty thousand were thought to be prisoners. It was not until American troops had actually arrived that we recognised that Australia was only one of the smaller nations in a worldwide struggle. We hated admitting it. We hated even more having to acknowledge that the conduct of this war, in which we had already lost sons, brothers, husbands and friends, was determined by three great powers: America (who had lost little to date), Britain and Russia, all of whom could dictate to us. Being only a part of the British Empire, we had no direct

149

representation. Where our men or our materials were sent was, to a degree, outside our control. And we were now standing in the greatest danger Australia had ever faced: we were preparing for invasion.

That the United States of America was now our ally was fine, but in the way that little things rankle and are apt to divert attention from the main topic – in this case survival – we loathed the American propaganda machine. Hollywood hit us, and we retaliated blindly against the only ambassadors we could see – the young, unscarred men so composedly taking over our cities. Humphrey Bogart, John Wayne and their like, winning the celluloid battles, were as much to blame as any other factor for our unspoken resistance to the American invasion of our homeland.

It wasn't always unspoken. When our proud 9th Division arrived home, and we saw them for the first time since they sailed in 1939 and won fame through the siege of Tobruk, the streets of our cities were thronged with Yanks, many with an Australian girl on their arm. The common description of our allies, 'over-paid, over-sexed and over here', was heard openly in the streets.

'What do you think of us stealing your girls?' the Americans asked the battle-toughened diggers.

'Aw, you didn't steal them,' a digger is said to have replied. 'You just sorted them out for us.'

By September 1943 there were one hundred and twenty thousand US army personnel actually in Australia, and an unknown number of air corps, as well as the thousands constantly 'staging' through the whole continent. They were concentrated in only a few centres and were highly visible. In Brisbane there were more men and women in uniform than the sub-tropical city had had civilians prior to the war. The vast numbers of Americans in the south-west Pacific area presented a great challenge. In addition to supplying its own army, Australia had to assist with supplying many of the needs of these servicemen, including food. Men and materials also had to be found for building roads, aerodromes, camps and hostels for those Americans within Australia.

On top of all this, the civilian population found it had to share with these men the limited wartime facilities of its cities – taxis, cinema tickets, cafés, rationed food, telephone services, office staff and local suppliers. Americans of all ranks had better-quality uniforms and twice the spending allowance of Australian servicemen. The Australian official history of the Second World War states: 'Their reputation as free spenders often won the Americans more than their share of the available amenities and this was frequently the cause of resentment.'

Whatever their differences, the two armies both fought in New Guinea, at the front door of Australia. New Guinea was a wilderness of unknown terrain compared with western Europe, where for a century professional armies had left a rich heritage of military and topographical information. Even data on the health problems and climatic conditions peculiar to the region was meagre. A

Opposite above: After the war broke out, the afternoon bridge parties held by Melbourne women became toy-making sessions for Britain's bombed-out children

Opposite below: During the war my father, a veteran of the First World War, kept a small timber line open in the Gippsland forests. Built for three light trains a week, it now carried heavy timber for war construction twice a day

Opposite: The small
plane is an essential
means of transport
across Australia's vast
distances, especially
for the Flying Doctor
service

few missionaries at odd times, and a few foot patrols, were the only traffic that 90 per cent of this huge island had ever seen.

The most lasting impression left from our partnership with America was gratitude for its ships having defeated the Japanese navy as they sailed through the Coral Sea at the approaches to Australia. A less happy memory was the slanting of news releases by MacArthur so as to favour America. When *we* won a battle the press called it: 'Allied victory!' When *his* men won, it was: 'American victory!' When the Japanese pushed us back over the Kokoda Trail in New Guinea he wrote: 'Australians in retreat', even though the Americans nearby were being defeated as soundly. When the Australians retaliated with a costly but victorious push and drove the Japanese back over the Kokoda Trail to the sea, again it was 'The Allies'. Never did he give us our just dues. We didn't want praise, but we hated having our men treated so shabbily. 'Allies rout Japanese!' the headlines cried when for the first time the Japanese were repulsed, defeated in a seaborne landing. It was at Milne Bay, and the defenders were Australian. The British soldier Viscount Slim wrote of them, 'Of all the Allies it was the Australian soldier who first broke the spell of invincibility of the Japanese Army.' Later General MacArthur's chiefs of staff wrote,

> The much publicized 'invincibility' of the Nipponese soldier had been blasted during the long campaign that started over the Kokoda Trail in New Guinea. He bled and died like any other mortal, but of late it had been found that he would surrender.

It was not only the men who served the country in the war. Women played a vital role at home and abroad, and it changed their status immeasurably. 'You can say what you like, but it does a man a world of good just to be able to look at a woman,' wrote one airman when the Royal Australian Air Force Nursing Service arrived in New Guinea. No one would deny the psychological effect, but they also worked hard, long hours in dangerous situations, and some of them paid the price. Sisters from the Australian Army Nursing Service served from Tobruk to the Pacific islands, with Greece and Crete thrown in. Along with the naval and air force sisters and enlisted VADs they were the only Australian women allowed to serve overseas until 1944. All but one of the nurses aboard the hospital ship *Centaur* died when, *en route* to New Guinea to pick up wounded in 1943, it was torpedoed a few miles off the Queensland coast. The newspapers echoed the cry of the people: 'The Ultimate Crime', they called it. Sister Vivian Bullwinckel was the sole survivor of a massacre on the beach at Banka Island. She was marched into the sea with twenty-one other nurses who had reached shore after the ship on which they were escaping from Singapore was bombed and sunk. All died of gunshot wounds in the back except this young woman who later struggled ashore, washed her wounds and lived for three and a half years in a prison camp, afraid that if her secret became

Right: Ayers Rock, one of Australia's most famous landmarks. To the Aborigines it is one of their sacred sites, which they believe are desecrated if touched by white men

Above right: 'It was one such torrent which almost carried our house away.'

Below right: 'A solemn, empty, dry flatness': a cyclone approaches

154

*In the Stirling Ranges of Western Australia
a road winds off apparently to infinity*

Alice Springs – 'an
embryonic Reno
whose rate of growth
is staggering'

Inset: Australia has
always been a nation
of immigrants. Thai
opal dealers examine
a prospector's finds

159

known she would be in danger as the only witness. She lived to give evidence at the War Crimes Trials in Japan in 1946.

Opposite: A modern gold mine at Bullfinch, Western Australia

When the first bombs fell just north of Australia, a matter of hours before Pearl Harbor was attacked, Prime Minister Curtin spoke on what we now called 'the radio' and bluntly told us that the honeymoon was over, and the real war was upon us. If Australia was to be saved, every man and woman was needed. 'Did he say every woman?' we asked. How ironic. Since 1938 women had trained at their own expense, had drawn up a national register of women willing and trained to serve – and had been told, officially, that they would only be required for 'relief and mercy work'. Some of us had enlisted in the nursing services early on, but of those young women who were anxious to join the navy, army and air force only a handful of specialists were taken. Among them were the signallers trained by a Sydney woman, Mrs Florence McKenzie, known as Mrs Mac. She turned out such superbly trained people that by early 1942 she was asked to train the Royal Australian Air Force signallers and some army and navy, as well as merchant navy men and senior American servicemen.

But now women were wanted to release men for the front line, and they came in droves until seventy thousand were in uniform. For most it was their first time away from home; it was still the age when girls left their father's house to go to their husband's house. In those pre-pill days it was the greatest experiment with women yet undertaken in Australia.

As well as the women in the three armed services there was a fourth service, the Australian Women's Land Army. Working far from the city streets where they could parade their uniforms, they toiled in unglamorous surroundings at sometimes unpleasant and almost always heavy physical work, usually for longer hours than the forty-eight-hour week then prevailing. Land Army shock troops were rushed to wherever they were needed: to Queensland to help harvest the cotton crop, to South Australia and Tasmania to pick fruit and work in the dried fruit factories, and to Western Australia to gather in the wheat harvest. They worked in the fruit, vegetable, dairying, flax, tobacco and cotton industries, in mixed farming, in poultry-raising and in pastoral industries. These intrepid women classed wool, picked roots, milked cows, fed pigs, drove tractors, mustered, yarded, killed and skinned sheep, cut chaff and crushed corn. Others qualified as certified herd testers. Helen Ising, who worked on the land at Evelyn Downs station in South Australia, wrote in 1944:

The only other employees are 20 odd blacks. The station is 700 square miles and runs 5000 sheep, as well as goats and lots of good horses. Shearing is in full swing now and my work consists mainly of piece-picking the wool and helping to class it, and yarding sheep.

I have done all sorts of things I've never done before, riding after horses at full gallop and going on 30- to 40-mile rides after lost horses, leaving home at mid-day and returning at eight or nine o'clock at night.

On the shoulders of these girls and women rested the responsibility of feeding the navy, army, air force and civilians of Australia and the US servicemen in Australia and the south-west Pacific.

As in other warring nations, women built aircraft and made machinery and ammunition. 'We were young, earnest, loyal and full of fun,' wrote Joan Dowson. They took over men's jobs, delivered ice, bread and milk, and manned butcher's shops and other establishments previously banned to them. It was the all-out war effort Curtin had demanded of us women. If some took advantage of the times and lived the social life to the hilt, the rest of us weren't too envious. When we saw their photographs in the social pages we'd just grin. After all, we too were living life to the full.

On 8 May 1945 the bells had been rung all over Australia as they were being rung in Europe. It was called VE Day – Victory in Europe. Germany had capitulated, Hitler had taken his own life, the doors of the concentration camps had been flung open by the Allies and revealed that the reasons for which we had fought this war – as opposed to the sordid trade wars of the past – were indeed vindicated for all time. For the first time we knew exactly what had happened to the Jews of Europe, to the gypsies and any others who did not fit the mould claimed to be superior to all others.

On 3 September, the bells rang out once more, but with such fervour this time that even in distant suburbs and in tiny country towns the sound was joyous. Women queued with men to peal the glad tidings on every little church bell. It had ended; it was VP Day – Victory in the Pacific; the war the Japanese had begun had finished. The living would come home, the lights would go on again all over the world.

At the end of the war we and our country were run down. In the 1940s our railways were still a prime necessity in this vast land, but now they were worn out. There had been little money during the Depression to spend on rolling stock, engines and tracks. Hard on the heels of that bad time came war, meaning even less replacement of tracks and engines and rolling stock that had had to be used in a way they were never made for.

My father, the old First World War man, spent the Second World War as flying ganger on a little line in the Gippsland forests which had been built at the turn of the century and normally carried a train three times a week for a few settlers and their produce. When war came timber was needed to build army barracks and so on, and long, heavy loads were hauled out twice a day. Dad had to 'run' the track on his pull trike each morning before the first train and then, after giving the all-clear that the rails were safe, ride on the engine to watch for rails bent in the hot summer sun. His flying gang were on twenty-four-hour standby.

On the major routes to the north, when the push was on against the Japanese I had seen – and at times been in – long troop trains on the way south, with

*Left: Gangers re-
laying a section of track
after a flood
Below: The little
inspection motor used
by my father on the
railway track*

returning men on leave or lightly injured patients, shunted into sidings for half a day at a time to let the northbound troop trains go through. At one period, in 1943, *all* southbound trains were cancelled to permit the urgently needed troops to be rushed to the northern front. Single-rail tracks across the arid lands of a lightly populated nation had borne vast armies across great distances and had left Australia's whole railway system exhausted.

In psychological terms the problems were perhaps even greater. The First World War had left us with widows and orphans after the loss of the fittest and best of our men, a debt that hung round our neck like an albatross avenging the blood sacrifice we had so willingly, wildly made. And what now did this war bequeath unto us? Not the lasting, undying pride we had felt amid the sadness that followed the first 'Great War'.

Certainly, as our men returned, yellow from the anti-malarial drug atabrin or shaking from the disease itself, riddled with three varieties of worm, emaciated through diarrhoea and amoebic dysentery, stinking with tropical ulcers and sores that had burst and soiled their clothes, we felt a solicitude. But apart from a few rare, death-defying and death-receiving stories there was little in our newspapers to help balance the plethora of material we had read of the Americans' part in this war at our own end of the world. The children born to our men who had been to this war would grow up in an aura of American war films and books that would swamp our output and quality. Indeed, the present generation of Australians speak of the Second World War starting on 7 December 1941, the day of Pearl Harbor.

Amongst those who came back were the survivors of the Japanese prison camps, and none of these men was unmarked. One-third of their number, we now realised, had died in the camps that stretched from Singapore through Thailand and Burma to Borneo and Japan. They had been used as slave labour in conditions that only a race who viewed their kind with disgust would inflict. This is what made these prisoners different from any others in past wars: the Japanese saw surrender as an act of total, unspeakable disgrace that only the most shameless would perform. From the highest rank to the lowest, Japanese soldiers and guards in the camps despised what they saw as less than human: men who would lay down their arms in preference to what the Japanese themselves saw as honourable death. It is a concept hard for Westerners to accept.

The brilliant tactics, training and tough physique of the Japanese army, allied to their devotion, bravery and unquestioning loyalty to their emperor-God, had brought them pell-mell down the jungles of Asia. Their initiative was such that they ran, walked, swam and cycled (on collapsible cycles so light that each man could carry his own, along with his own rice ration). They over-ran the British army, of which the Australians were a part, and General Percival ordered his army to surrender. 'We were told to lay down our arms,' the survivors repeated.

For three weeks at the beginning of the war with Japan this corner of the
British and Dutch Empires had been a turmoil of men and women attempting
to escape on ships that were sunk almost as soon as they reached them – some
nurses and civilians were bombed off as many as three ships; others, in tiny
boats, were swept towards palm-fringed island shores only to be swept out to
sea by coastal currents and never seen again. Wreckage swept on to beaches
and was swept away again by the next tide. Men swimming from one sunken
ship got on floats from another going down.

Apart from a mass of such stories Australia was aware soon after the end of
the war that there was another, darker side to such a vast experience. Those
who had come back from the camps had walked a strange, eerie death-trail for
almost the whole of their war service, and this would always set them apart.
Theirs was a further edge of that mateship that all soldiers experience. They
had literally supported one another's bodies through travail; they had held one
another in pain, fear and death and after death had carried the bodies of friends
to the cholera pit or fire; they had carried the bundle of bones that had once
been a man to a shallow grave beside the railway they built through Thailand
to Burma. It was a calvary that belongs to the barbaric times we had thought
were past.

As always, small communities saw the matter most clearly. From Numurkah,
the small town nearest to our railway siding at Waaia, twelve men from a
single regiment were captured. A girl friend once said to me, 'I suppose, by the
law of averages, I danced with half those men in the 1930s. I only hope I danced
well.' It seemed to me to sum up that feeling we of that generation have of
never being able to come to grips with what happened to those lost battalions.
We feel a sort of communal guilt that we put them in a position in which they
were beaten, locked in cages, starved, dehydrated, their teeth knocked out, bones
broken, stomachs bloated with raw rice and water. The men of many nations
were treated similarly, but these were our men. We have never forgotten it.

Escape was rarely possible – natives killed many who attempted to steal boats;
and there was little scope for heroics. The writer Donald Stuart – bushman,
horseman, miner and outback drover – remains in the eyes of many the typical
Australian larrikin, even in the death camps. Sir Edward E. Dunlop, the well-
known surgeon who also worked on the infamous Burma Railway, described
him:

Naked, except for bits and pieces strung round him like bizarre decorations,
half a hat on his straw hair, he'd stalk past Japanese officers, refusing to salute.
He was forever getting bashed up because of this. Yet every time he passed
me his arm flashed up in the snappiest salute you ever saw.

We now knew that a shift in old ties, old loyalties was upon us. Britain could
not again even pretend to be Mother England defending her cubs. The war had

left her stricken physically and financially, but beyond that we knew that the days of sending a gunboat up a river were over. The power of the once invincible Royal Navy was ended. We had learned that early in the war in the Pacific, when direct hits from Japanese aircraft had sunk the mighty *Repulse* and *Prince of Wales*.

Breaking old ties comes hard, even though we had seen the feet of clay at Suvla Bay in 1915. But we all have feet of clay, and it was childish to have believed our Mother England was exempt. Still, the break left us in confusion. We admired America, but could never love her as we had thought we loved England.

Opposite above: The desert of my childhood – Sunset Country, where for a thousand miles men had to seek waterholes known only to Aborigines

Opposite below: After the war three hopefuls pile their gear into the boot of their car, off to join a mini-gold rush in the town of Wedderburn, Victoria

Never the lotus closes,
Never the wild fowl wake,
But a soul goes out on the east wind
That died for England's sake.

We had been taught this poem at school in the 1930s, and many of us were even then willing to be one of these souls. But now time and change had pitched us into a void out of which we must climb.

Some historians say our relationship with England changed during the Second World War. I believe it had been constantly changing since the first day free settlers arrived: they had not come so far, said goodbye to loved ones forever, to live under the same restrictions they had left behind them. The early unions showed that, in particular the shearers with their spread across the land, and those impractical people who fled to Paraguay. When the Japanese attacked north of Australia early in 1942 we knew the romance had ended. Yet none of these events in themselves, or together, totally set us apart.

The real reason was that we had grown up. We had done well at what was praiseworthy in those days: we'd fought and faced the wilderness, we'd sent our sons to die – in the belief that this was how a nation is created and survives. We cut ourselves away from the apron-strings of Mother England, and apart from the colourful, spectacular pageantry and historical ties we were on our own, to stand or fall by our own decisions.

We began to question ourselves as we had never done before. Why had we permitted ourselves always to be a minor part of some other army, never acting independently – given the fact that Australia had produced (according to the British Prime Minister, Lloyd George) the greatest colonial commander of the First World War, General Monash, whose strategy and leadership helped bring about the defeat of the Germans in 1918? Like people in other countries, we began to think about the place we lived in. Were we husbanding it well? What were we doing to the land? To the Aboriginals? The exigencies of pioneering days were past; we must now put our moral affairs in order.

In 1945 Mary Gilmore had written in *The Worker* reminding us that this war

would soon be over and our men would come home. She foresaw Australia opening her doors to all-comers, displaced persons, refugees and those who for one reason or another needed a new home. She welcomed the idea, yet she issued a warning: 'Their traditions and culture will swamp over ours as being more romantic in distance. But,' she urged us to remember, 'ours are ours.' Her heart wept at the possibility that we would come to a time when we said, '*Vale, Gundagai.*'

We assisted over three hundred thousand Italians to emigrate from their workless homeland in six years. Soon we would boast, in Melbourne, the third largest community of Greeks outside Athens and Salonika. People of sixty-seven nationalities – including, in recent years, a preponderance of Asians – have taken over whole streets and suburbs in all capital cities. Fares, food and lodgings were paid for, jobs found, medical and social welfare and community assistance given. All are encouraged to speak their own language, fly their own flag, follow their own religion, and observe their own culture and traditions. Since the Second World War we have taken in more immigrants per capita than any country in the world except Israel.

Those of us born in Australia of Australian-born parents are now, I suppose, an ethnic minority. Time will tell if this mix was wise; many of us, looking at our seventh-generation Australian grandchildren with their golden skin or the cheekbones of a race once 'foreign' to us, believe it will be magnificent. Our generosity as a nation will be repaid. The cost may be that we have indeed obliterated the track back to Gundagai. Few now know the scent of gum blossom, the colloquial language has been buried in dictionaries, and the old days exist as film. But change we must have if we are to survive down here. And though we may never do so again, we *did* once ride down that track to Gundagai. We know it, and believe it gives the strength of a backbone to our land.

The Mythological Crucible

ROBYN DAVIDSON

I was born in 1950 in the one-horse hospital of Miles, our nearest town, twenty-five miles away. It was a good year for Virgos, Robyns and wars, both hot and cold. The bumper crop of September births is easy enough to explain. The deprivations of the Pacific war were beginning to fade from memory, and there was enough money around not only to send care packages to England (a country my forbears had not seen for several generations but which some of them continued to call 'home'), but also to lash out on enough cold beer around the Yuletide season to forget about the importance of contraception. The burgeoning quantity of Robyns born in that decade remains a mystery.

At about the time I was being conceived, and myxomatosis was being introduced to exterminate the rabbit plague nibbling away at the roots of Australia's economy, a new government was being sworn in, to replace the Labor government which had seen Australia through the final years of the war. It was led by a bushy-eyebrowed man who rode to power on the promise of exterminating the Communist Party, which, according to him, was also decimating Australia's economy. It began what is known to history as the Menzies Era, sixteen years of it followed by a further seven years of conservative rule – the Big Sleep. According to my parents he was a shining statesman, a witty speaker, a father figure who knew what was best for us. He was the good shepherd, who coaxed his bleating public into the safe pastures of economic prosperity and protected it from the dingo-like ravages of the Yellow Peril. He loved the Queen. He loved cricket. He was, above all, safe. There are other interpretations however. As an acquaintance of mine put it recently: 'Menzies was a poisonous old fart, hanging around the backside of Great Britain.' As the word 'fart' had never been heard in our household, I adhered, in my youth, to my parents' view.

We lived, my mother, father, sister and I, on a small – by Queensland standards – cattle property called Stanley Park. Even then the name seemed inappropriate to me. Parks were things which existed in places called London or Europe and they had oak trees and daffodils, fairies and Peter Pan. Rarely did we receive enough rain to turn the yellows and ochres of the Downs country into a poor excuse for green, or to send a muddy torrent choked with topsoil, bloated cattle and torn-up river gums down the wide, white creek bed which passed beside our house. It was one such torrent which almost carried our house away, and caused my father to sit on the front steps with his head in his hands, contemplating his losing battle with the bush and the bank. For us children, the thunderstorm was the most thrilling event in our lives. Hail lay a foot thick where once there had been dry grass and bluebells. Joyously we filled buckets with these miracles of ice, while our parents discussed 'selling up'.

Although I left Stanley Park when I was four, I remember, like a taste or a smell, a forlorn, deserted quality the country had. It was as if loneliness seeped out of the soil into the bright, brazen light. But of course, that was a projection on my part, brought about, perhaps, by a guilty race conscience. Not far from where we lived a group of blacks had been murdered in a dry river bed fifty years before – a common enough occurrence during the dark ages of Australian history, which began in 1788 and continued until 1928, when the last recorded massacre of Aboriginal families took place. So carefully had my antecedents obliterated history that I knew nothing of this at the time. It would be many years before I discovered the rot which riddled white Australia's history, beneath the evasions, silences and lies, and longer still before an Australian Prime Minister would say: 'More than any foreign aid programme, more than any international obligation we meet or forfeit, more than any part we may play in any treaty or alliance, Australia's treatment of her Aboriginal people will be the thing upon which the rest of the world will judge Australia and Australians – not just now, but in the greater perspective of history.'

Our house was a typical bush homestead – rambling, ramshackle and set up on stilts to keep it cool. A succession of blue cattle dogs were chained up under the tank stand. A hardy variety of bougainvillea blazed along the peeling weatherboard walls; welcome swallows made their homes under the corrugated iron roof; deadly snakes made theirs in the woodpile. A succession of black and white cats prowled a wide veranda gauzed in by a fine wire mesh which, while effectively shutting out most of the relieving breezes of sundown, was no match for the squadrons of insects which kamikazed by the million each night into the hurricane lamps. It was these kinds of domestic difficulties – the spiders'

Opposite above: A typical bush home-stead – 'rambling, ram-shackle and set up on stilts to keep it cool'

Opposite below: 'We were unprepared ... for our first visit to a "fair dinkum" city'. In the wealthiest suburbs, every back yard seemed to have its swimming pool

webs, the powdery dust, the piles of desiccating insects, the stray snakes and the lack of those modern appliances like vacuum cleaners and electric irons which littered the kitchens of her city chums – which caused my mother to sit on the back steps with her head in her hands.

Or perhaps it was the isolation which got her down. Her view, from those back steps, was of never-ending sameness. A solemn, empty, dry flatness with no distant mountains, no dazzling streams, no rich greens to relieve the eye. Yellows, sepias, drab bluey-greys stretched away to meet the empty blue vault, which bleached out as the day progressed and the sun crushed the vitality out of everything. One hundred years before, the explorer Ludwig Leichhardt – hero of Patrick White's novel *Voss* – passed across our land on his second attempt to cross Australia from east to west. He carved a large L into a tree up in our brigalow forest before disappearing forever into the same oblivion which yawned before my mother's eyes. She was a city woman, used to an exciting social life. In her youth she had sung in operas, dressed herself up in chiffon and flowers and danced like Isadora Duncan. Oddly, my strongest image of her comes from a time before my birth. She described to me how, as a young woman, she had gone on a picnic with friends, and they had all decorated each other and the car with wild flowers. There were very few wild flowers at Stanley Park.

Our nearest neighbour lived three miles away. Our closest link with Elsewhere was the siding at Gulugaba – a tin shed beside the railway line. At the end of the long, rutted track in front of our house was a tin box on a stump, into which, once a week, were placed letters full of news and tacit sympathy from my mother's coast-clinging relatives: she was grateful for both. The wireless was our only other contact with the faraway world of events. Sometimes the cicadas and crickets were so loud that we had to turn it up to hear our favourite children's programme, *The Argonauts*, or our favourite serial, *Blue Hills*, or the Sunday play. When it came to news time my father moved his chair closer, cupped his hand over a war-damaged ear, puffed on his pipe and listened avidly. He may well have heard Menzies proclaim:

> The world is full of danger.... China which we perhaps once regarded as an ancient and inactive country is in course of becoming a great power under the sternest Communist control. It seeks to expand, to divide and to conquer. ... Does any Australian sensibly believe that the defence of Australia's existence (because existence as a free country is what matters) would not be challenged if the Communists over-ran South-East Asia, subverted Indonesia and stood at the very threshold of our northern door?
>
> The simple English of this matter is that with our vast territory and our small population we cannot survive a surging Communist challenge from abroad except by the co-operation of powerful friends....

Twenty-five years later I would discover that, in the most remote areas of

Australia, graziers were still preparing themselves for imminent invasion by little yellow people from the north. There was a drought on at the time, and the owners of cattle stations were hopping into their private Cessnas to fly to Canberra and demand drought relief. One of the reasons they gave to Parliament was that, if they had to walk off their properties, there would be no one left in the desert areas to defend the country against the Chinese. The idea that one gallant little family a hundred miles away from the next gallant little family could, by firing off their shotguns at the hordes emerging from the heat mirage along the horizon, save Australia from Communist takeover, might have been funny, if the gallant little families had not taken it so seriously.

Before his election Menzies had broadened his Liberal Party's essentially urban base by forming a coalition with the Country Party, thereby securing my dad's vote. He blamed Communist influence in the trade unions for the protracted and bitter strikes in the railways, on the waterfront and down the coalmines – strikes which presented the Labor Party with a dilemma. On the one side, conservative forces clamoured for law and order; on the other, radicals fumed at the government's disciplining of strikers, particularly when troops were sent in during the coalminers' strike of 1949. Similarly, the right wing of the party and the Catholics did not want Labor to recognise the People's Republic of China; the left wing demanded that it be recognised immediately. Menzies capitalised on these divisions and cleverly exploited fear of the Reds. The Communists provided him with a means to weaken the trade union movement and remove opposition to the demands of the country's new economic masters.

Australians, suddenly aware that they lived in one of the richest countries in the world, were obsessed with making money. They were fed up with the controls imposed by the war, with the growing number of civil servants in the federal capital, and with the strikers who, having suffered through the Depression and a war, wanted their share of the cake. Menzies had already proved himself a champion of war. In 1948, the year before he came to power, he had suggested the use of nuclear weapons to break the Berlin blockade. Then, in 1951, he announced that Australia would be at war again within three years. He was to send troops to Malaya and Borneo and, of course, to Vietnam. And in the year of my birth he committed Australia's armed forces to the great ideological conflict in Korea, in which Australia suffered nearly two thousand casualties. His Communist Party Dissolution Act was disallowed by the High Court in 1950, but the following year he attempted to obtain, by referendum, powers to deal with the Communists and to alter the Conciliation and Arbitration Act. The referendum was narrowly defeated, after a courageous campaign in favour of political liberty by the leader of the opposition, H. V. Evatt. I do not know how my parents voted. I do know that to them, and to most people like them, Communism had replaced Fascism as the great world evil, and it was poised to take over Australia.

Above: Prime Minister Robert Menzies blamed Communist influence in the trade unions for the string of post-war strikes. Marx House, the Sydney headquarters of the party, being raided by police

Left: A meeting called by the Communists during the miners' strike of 1949

Every night when the news was over my father was available for bedtime stories. My sister and I sat beside him listening, enthralled, to tales of distant and romantic Africa, neither of us imagining that we too lived in a distant and romantic land. While my mother had been surviving the Depression my father had been wandering around the Dark Continent in a pith helmet, mining for gold, going on safari and, I suspect, poaching a bit of ivory. My strongest image of him comes from two photographs – in one of them he is wading through waist-deep muddy water, holding a harpoon in his hand; in the next he is standing with his foot on the back of an enormous crocodile. He would speak of Africa wistfully, and perhaps it was because both my parents yearned to be somewhere else that I grew up restless and uncertain of where my home was. For despite the domesticity and hard work which rooted us to the various places in which we lived, they all had a temporary quality, as if we were waiting on the outskirts of something to which we would eventually belong. Or perhaps that is how many white Australians feel, like transplants who haven't quite taken root.

My parents' marriage was mixed: that is, she was urban, he rural. She was from the aspiring lower-middle class, which took pains to cover up any convict ancestry. He was from the landed squattocracy, which took pride in a non-convict ancestry. The love affair was legalised during the romance of war, and their wedding photo shows a deliriously happy couple – he in sergeant's uniform, she in tasteful crepe suit and a net fascinator which did not obscure the light of adoration in her eyes. I can well understand the attraction. She was all daintiness and grace and bubbling wit. He was all Errol Flynn. He was forty when they married; she was twenty-four. He had sailed back from Africa in a thirty-six-foot schooner and his eyes were the colour of the sea. Such is the stuff of grand passion.

But the stultifying niceness, the snug conservatism and the grasping materialism of the fifties left little room for that kind of romance. Excitement and adventure gave way to settling down, growing prosperous and raising publicly happy nuclear families even if it killed you. After the intensity of war, life must sometimes seem pallid to those who survive it. No doubt there were many people who felt, but could not explain, a certain hollowness in their lives which even the advent of swizzle sticks, plastic roses and light-weight irons could not fill.

Children somehow construct the truth out of whispers and secrets. Just as I could feel the undercurrents of discontent which ran beneath the wholesomeness of family life, so I could smell the acrid remains of war, like smoke from a spent bush fire. The rare growling of a DC3 overhead would send me scuttling under the house to escape the bombs which must inevitably fall. And there were other, more subtle, anxieties. My father was almost a dead war hero. A friend of his, Ivan Lyon, had led a small group of hand-picked men into a Japanese harbour in the dead of night to place bombs on the hulls of enemy ships. The success of their mission demanded a repeat run. He contacted my father, who was eager to go but, being fortyish and having suffered two hernias already, not to mention blackwater fever, was regretfully deemed physically unfit. Ivan and all his crew were captured and beheaded by the Japanese. 'Who – and for that matter, where – would I be,' I often thought, 'if Poppy had died in the war?' When old age had made him wise, his reminiscences of war heroism changed dramatically. Once, he described his shelling of a tank in Tobruk. A soldier had come out of the tank on fire. 'A human torch,' said my father, quickly blinking away tears. His fondest memory was of drinking beer with enemy Italians on Christmas Day. But during my childhood Jerries and Japs were the bad guys and war seemed like a game.

My mother's patriotic fervour manifested itself in a horror at the Japanese products which were beginning to flood the market. With pursed and disapproving lips she would check the bottoms of cups to see if they bore that terrible brand 'Made in Japan'. The same disapproval was reserved for some German neighbours of ours, who had been interned during the war years and were still unpopular in the community. Whether they were Nazi sympathisers or not, their guttural accents would ensure that they remained unpopular long after Japanese gadgets became ideologically desirable. Japan, after all, was soon to become a major buffer zone against the Communists. But bitter though my mother may have been towards the enemy, she did not gloss over the devastations of war. 'Their faces were green, pea green,' she once whispered, her face full of pain. She was describing corpse-like American soldiers, returning from the Pacific, marching through the streets of her home town.

It is not surprising that an emotional dulling, a deadening of the imagination, like shell shock, pervaded the post-war decade. Australia had seen the world and become linked to its fate, and the fate of the world was in question. I was two years old when the wind changed direction off the Monte Bello Islands and blew radioactive material from Britain's first nuclear bomb across the Australian continent.

Like most women of the fifties, my mother was not immune to the barrage of propaganda designed to get females out of the workforce and back into the home. They had done their duty for the war effort by occupying the vacuum left by the fighting men and entering the world of production. Now their duty was to dismount graciously from their tractors and get on with the proper business of reproduction. Women's magazines were crammed with stories of selfless housewives giving up their talents, their passions, their ambitions for the sake of love, marriage, family. Recently I re-read a batch of them, and the propaganda is so blatant that it is difficult to believe that women of the time were not conscious of being manipulated. One story which particularly struck me was that of a woman artist who decides to enter a painting in a competition. She knows that it is her best work yet, and that she is sure to win. But her creative effort takes time away from her husband, who becomes sulky and

Right: American servicemen seemed very glamorous to many Australian women.
Below: These Australians, being liberated by US Marines, had been prisoners of the Japanese for over three years

morose. In the end she throws the painting in a puddle, and as she watches the colours dribble down the canvas she feels an enormous relief and a sudden joy. So, one imagines, does hubbie.

Contemporary Australia has a reputation for producing tough-minded women. Indeed, tough-minded women are one of our principal exports. In a culture whose misogyny has deep historical roots, and in which women were traditionally regarded as something like a cross between a sheep and a kitchen appliance, it is only to be expected that daughters of fifties' mothers should have produced an Antipodean feminism with a sharp cutting edge.

White women were not the only ones shuffled up and down the economic ladder by the vagaries of war. While Aborigines in Western Australia were being prevented from moving south of the twentieth parallel (the 'leper line'), and still others were being gaoled as 'potential enemies', some of their more fortunate relations in the centre and the north were being employed on war construction projects. They did not yet have the vote, but for the first time they did receive decent wages and housing. Aboriginal women, too, were brought from the forgotten settlements of the outback to work as domestics in the city – that is, to occupy those jobs which white women could now afford to vacate. Most of those black women had never seen a town, let alone a city. They were forced to leave family and country behind. Traumatic it may have been, but when the war ended so did six years of money and relative comfort. Many did not want to return to the bottom of the barrel. They had little choice.

My mother appeared to accept her post-war role without anger, fully expecting the happiness promised her by all the happy endings of all the stories in all the women's magazines. She became, in true Australian tradition, a civilising influence on rough and ready rural life.

She taught primary school lessons to my sister via the correspondence system. She was both nurse and doctor to us, because there were no nurses or doctors within cooee. She learned how to pull cattle from bogs, strain fencing wire, chop wood and be alone for days on end. On her treadle Singer she sewed dresses with ruffles, pintucks and puffed sleeves. She polished the cracked floorboards of the dining room until you could see your face in them. She dug a garden and coaxed silverbeet, our staple green, out of the dry, unyielding earth. From the basics of weevilly flour, salt beef and sugar she brought forth culinary masterpieces of the strictly English type. On Mondays she washed everything by hand, rinsed it in Bluo and starched it, ready for Tuesday – the day for damping down, plonking irons on the top of the Kooka wood stove, and sweating over each flounce and tuck while the temperature climbed into the hundreds. She read us books, scrimped to buy us an encyclopaedia from a travelling salesman, and encouraged us to sing around the piano of a Saturday evening. She threaded ribbons in our hair, and lobbied our father for one or two train trips to that remote and unimaginable place, the city. She fed the lean, ragged, dried-up swagmen who still arrived at our door from time to

Left: At work in a canning factory. After the war, most women had to relinquish their paid jobs to the returning troops, and go back to domestic life

Left: Menzies was a champion of war, sending Australians to fight in both Malaya and Vietnam. Accompanying the troops to Malaya was a party of nurses

time, looking for bit work or tucker. She learned to lie convincingly to the dodgy strangers who came and leered and asked if she were alone. 'My husband will be back directly,' she would say, holding the snarling dog by the collar.

But she never managed to lose her snake phobia. Even getting to the dunny at night was an expedition fraught with danger. Tiger snakes, king browns, western browns and copperheads were too much for my mother's fertile imagination. Having negotiated the path with much beating of long grass and peering down with the lantern, there were still the redbacks to contend with. Pretty little relatives of the black widow spider, these creatures chose, as their favourite hunting ground, the underside of the lid of the loo.

Life in the bush was full of such hazards. I was much too young to remember when our first car replaced the horse and dray. But I do dimly recall the day we drove the Austin through bush fires, and my sister and I almost expired. Wet cloths were pressed to our skin as the flames along the side of the road cracked open gum trees as if they were penny fireworks.

That my family's bank balance was not rocketed into the black by the economic boom was not the fault of the boom. My father was an excellent amateur astronomer, geologist and naturalist. He was a spinner of yarns, a talented craftsman and a dreamer. But his whimsical attitude to life, his gentleness and his deeply held Victorian values meant that he lacked the qualities needed for getting rich quick – chicanery, judgment and competitiveness. He also lacked luck. Wool prices were soaring; my father owned cattle. Minerals were being unearthed everywhere; my father neglected to buy shares. Like returning soldiers from the First World War, who had been given plots of barren land infested with an Australian native tree called mallee (if Gallipoli hadn't killed them, the mallee would), my father took up land which was choked with forests of brigalow. Without the capital with which to improve the property, hire labour or invest in one of the American tractors which were proliferating across the landscape like flies, his efforts at improvement were about as effective as scratching at a diamond. Off he would go before sun-up, with his stock whip, dog and axe, his packed lunch, thermos of tea and the whistle of an optimist, to saddle his horse. At night he would come home reeking of sweat, pleased with an honest day's work, whereupon he would sit with his legs up and ruminate on the wonders of nature and the beauty and mystery of the stars, while my mother heated water on the Kooka for his bath, made restless tapping sounds with her fingers, and gave out exasperated little sighs. Even after the fourth strangulated hernia he refused to admit defeat.

'Five and you're dead,' said the doctors.

'Load of bunkum,' said my father, smiling reassuringly through a barrage of exasperated sighs. He was to prove the doctors wrong.

The year 1954 was a very big one for us all. Previously, it seemed, nothing had ever changed. My dad's boots always sat by the front door. The yapping of the cattle dog and the clanking of corrugated iron in the wind were incessant.

Out in the bush my mother 'taught primary school lessons to my sister via the correspondence system'. These children, of the next generation, attend the School of the Air, doing their lessons by two-way radio

On Saturday, a boiled lolly was inevitably doled out by my mother's hand. Even when the bush fires came, or the hail made our house look like a Christmas card, even when my father lay doubled up with another hernia, or came home on his horse twice his normal size because he had ridden into a nest of wasps – even these momentous events were fixed in a bedrock of sameness. But in 1954 not only did the Queen pay her first visit to her Australian subjects, not only did the name Petrov strike fear and loathing into many Australian hearts, not only did the Labor Party begin to self-destruct, but the Davidson family crossed the aptly named Great Dividing Range, leaving the western slopes forever.

The long drive from Gulugaba to Mooloolah was undoubtedly hot, dusty and fraught with tensions, and I'm glad I don't remember it. What I do dimly recall was standing pressed close to my mother in a very crowded street, waving a little flag at a big black car. A lady with a pretty hat was waving back. Books may not have been a big feature in many Australian homes at the time, but invariably, alongside the Bible and the Children's Encyclopaedia, there would be a pop-up picture book of the coronation. Mothers dreamed secretly that their daughters would get hitched to Prince Charles. The Queen's hats were copied by milliners all over the country. Such intense royalism has left its mark in the subconscious minds of ordinary Australians. I know very few people who haven't dreamt that some member of the royal family visited them for a cuppa or a sexual encounter.

Menzies, that wily old anglophile, encouraged it all and stressed Australia's loyalty to the British Empire. But while tugging his forelock embarrassingly at Her Majesty with one hand, he was busily severing military and economic attachment to the mother country with the other. It was to be America who would take the place of Britain as our 'powerful friend'. For people like my father, who believed that British imperialism was the source of all virtue, the changeover and the clamouring after American junk which was beginning to afflict us all were sources of some bemusement. 'Still,' he would say, 'the Yanks saved us during the war and we've got to have progress.'

We were as helpless at protecting ourselves from America's money, gadgetry and ideals, as the Aborigines had been at protecting themselves from the flu. But unlike the Aborigines, we welcomed our invaders with open arms. 'Come, take, exploit,' we said, 'only give us your trinkets and teach us to jitterbug.'

Our love of America and our veneration for the royal family were matched in intensity only by our fear of the Red Menace. Twelve days after waving farewell to his adored Queen, Menzies announced that a member of the Russian Embassy staff in Canberra, Vladimir Petrov, wanted political asylum and had given evidence of an alleged Communist spy network in Australia. Shock horror headlines, and photos of a distressed Mrs Petrov being bullied by two KGB thugs at Darwin airport, filled the front pages for days. Menzies called for a royal commission into Soviet espionage. Reputations were being demolished all over the place, particularly within the Labor Party.

The Queen and Petrov provided Menzies with two ace cards, and when the elections came soon afterwards he remained firmly in office. A year later, the royal commission announced that no one was to be prosecuted, and there were (and still are) those who believed that the whole affair was a plot dreamed up by Australia's security service and the government. But by then the leader of the opposition, Dr Evatt, who had appeared as defence counsel before the Petrov Commission, was under attack from a powerful Catholic-based faction within his own party. From the resultant schism the Democratic Labor Party emerged, which promised to make Australia safe from Reds. In fact, by giving preferential voting to the Liberal-Country Party coalition, it made Australia safe for Menzies. The Labor Party's electoral prospects were severely weakened for many years to come.

The Great Dividing Range runs all the way down the eastern coast of the continent, separating wet from dry, urban from outback, dense population from thin. It also divides reality from myth, for while the early settlers huddled along the thin strip of coast, looking longingly across the seas to the real world, it was the dry country, the open, empty spaces of the interior which white Australians, the most urbanised population in the world, chose as their mythological crucible – a place where mateship, masculinity, xenophobia and philistinism were mixed to form the old stereotype we know and dislike so well, and which does not, and never did, do justice to the complexity of that elusive, problematical thing, national identity. But more of *Crocodile Dundee* later.

The village of Mooloolah boasted an industrial centre (one sleepy saw-mill), a shopping centre (one tiny post office which doubled as a general store) and a cultural centre (one Methodist church a bit bigger than the dunny at Stanley Park, one derelict School of Arts Hall, and a primary school in which two teachers taught anything from fifteen to forty pupils, depending on the weather). I suppose all of us in that little community were pioneers of a kind. There was no building in the area more than thirty years old. We were part of a new wave, doing what our ancestors had done before us in other parts of the country – clearing bushland and preparing it for an invasion of groundsel, prickly pear, lantana, bracken, Pattersons's curse and Scotch thistles. It was the super-phosphates which gave the paddocks their sheen of English green.

Perhaps my mother thought, when she saw the lush kaikuyu pastures of our new home, that her husband's business acumen had taken a turn for the better. A sign proclaiming 'Malabah' in bold letters swung from a high wooden gate, behind which stood the big white house on the hill. Away from the house rolled two hundred acres of emerald paddocks, laced with babbling brooks and dotted with trees which looked like trees, and with sheep. We were a mere sixty miles from Brisbane, and the Pacific beaches lay twelve miles to the east. There was electricity, an ox-heart mango tree, rampant alamanda vines and an inside lav. I know that, as far as my mother was concerned, Malabah had one

attribute which surpassed all others. Tiger snakes, copperheads, western browns and king browns all lived on the other side of the Great Divide.

'Can you tell me what Mooloolah means?' my mother asked vivaciously after introducing herself to the store owner and postmaster.

'Abo word. Means red-bellied black snake. Poisonous buggers.'

The place was riddled with them. They dangled from the rafters of my cubby house. They slithered through the floorboards of the laundry. They sunned themselves on the passionfruit vine. They entered my mother's nightmares. It would not be long before she would be sitting on the back steps of our new home with her head in her hands, muttering that Malabah was nothing but a white elephant. It was such a poetic description of the solid, comfortable old house that at the time I could not understand her bitterness.

It is not exactly correct to say that Australia rode on the sheep's back. It rode on the Merino's back. My father's unerring instinct for failure had led him to buy Romney Marsh and Border Leicester sheep. English sheep. Sheep which found the steamy fecundity of the sub-tropics a less than ideal environment. Sheep which suffered from footrot, staggers, worm infestations, pink-eye, flyblown rumps, tumours and the kind of stupidity which led them to die in large numbers during the floods, which might cover half the property during the wet, or in the bush fires, which might destroy the other half during the dry, and to get themselves tangled up in the six-foot-high dingo-proof netting fences to which my father dedicated several more hernias and through which the wild dogs inevitably found their way.

Opposite: 'It is sometimes forgotten that Australia is a land of immigrants.' Immigrant families arriving by ship at Sydney (above), and Asian children on a Melbourne street (below)

There is a debate in Australia, between conservationists and farmers, concerning the eating habits of the native-born dingo. From my own experience I would say that a pure-bred dingo will rarely, if ever, attack a lamb. But domestic dogs who have gone feral, or dog–dingo crosses, will disembowel a whole flock for the sheer joy of it. We lost sixty of our two hundred sheep in one night. They lay scattered across the paddocks like bits of bloodied cotton wool. My father put them out of their misery with a bullet to the brain. The optimistic whistling and the exasperated sighs were back with a vengeance.

But for all our money worries, we were rich in comparison with our neighbours, and our dilapidated three-bedroom house could only be seen as luxurious when compared to the one-room shacks in which many of the dairy farmers and their families lived. Their holdings were too small ever to make a profit, and their lives consisted of never-ending work just to make ends meet. The children would be up by four in the morning, bringing in the cows for milking. After school they would hurry home, sometimes many miles, on their ponies or on foot for more of the same. What was most astonishing to me was that many of the farmers did not speak English very well.

It is sometimes forgotten that Australia is a land of immigrants. If it has become chic to find a convict ancestor, it is because there just aren't that many. The gold rush of the previous century attracted the first great wave, increasing the population threefold. Between the end of the Second World War and the early seventies three million came. As with previous intakes, preference was given to the British, 90 per cent of whom received assisted passage. But this time Europeans formed over half of the new arrivals.

Workers feared competition in the labour market. Protestants worried about an inundation of 'Micks'. Jews feared the arrival of Nazi sympathisers. Leftists were concerned at the conservatism of new arrivals who had suffered such trauma in Europe and who now wanted, above all, safety and stability. Menzies, who after the war continued Labor's policy of large-scale immigration, assured them of both. Previously there had been only Abos and Chinks for Anglo-Saxon Australians to feel superior to. Now there were Italians, Greeks, Poles, Yugoslavs, Finns – a smorgasbord for the xenophobe. It was a begrudging and suspicious population that greeted the new arrivals, some of whom had been crammed into ships like sheep, without water for washing and without adequate food. Perhaps this was when the Poms gained a reputation for 'whingeing'.

By 1951, 170,000 new Australians, or, as they were called variously by the old Australians, 'wops, wogs, poms, dagos, balts, huns and reffos', had been brought in, on the understanding that they would spend two years working in the heavy industries, the most important of which was the Snowy Mountains hydro-electric scheme – the grandest project Australia had ever undertaken. I well remember the feeling of pride that was generated along with the electricity. My father showed me newspaper photos of white water gushing down a mountain, of vast power stations, of eighty miles of tunnels under Mount Kosciusko – Australia's highest peak. This great engineering feat was symbolic of post-war prosperity and achievement and thousands of European immigrants worked on it.

By the time we arrived in Mooloolah many of the new Australians had begun to spread out into country areas. Our closest neighbour and friend was a Pole. He owned a Land Rover and a small pineapple farm skirting the precipitous slopes of infertile hills. In all the time I knew him, Ted never quite managed to master the English language. But it didn't matter. We adored each other, and who needs conversation for that. He brought me freshly crushed pineapple juice, and when he smiled his whole face wrinkled up in a most delightful way. Later on, his wife arrived fresh as a rose from Scotland. Like my parents, they had met as a consequence of war and it had taken Ted all this time to provide a home for her.

I remember quite clearly the day he finished building his shack ready for her arrival. It was simply the best cubby house I had ever seen – twenty foot square, with a neat double bed, a sink and a wood stove. Outside on the gritty white soil lay stacks of empty crates in which the pineapples would be sent south to the Golden Circle cannery. Beside them were mounds of pineapple tops, reeking and ready for planting. It is likely that Bunty regarded her new home with less enthusiasm than I. When Ted brought her to meet us she sat in the Land Rover with a dazed, uncomprehending look on her face, as if she had just landed on Mars. My mother's heart bled for her.

Bunty had skin that was almost transparent, and so soft it looked as if a powder puff would scratch it. The sandflies and mosquitoes smelt her Scottish blood a mile off and zoomed in for the kill. She could not resist scratching at the red welts which made her ankles and legs swell, and then turned septic. In the height of summer both of them would be out chipping the pines: that is, walking along the rows, hoeing weeds – thousands of weeds, miles of rows. The serrated leaves of the pines scratched at her legs and arms and gave her tropical ulcers. The skin of her hands split and cracked and the acid juice stung and burned them.

What, I wonder, had she expected of the 'lucky country'? An exotic South Seas paradise, dripping with wealth, where the ravaged of the world could find peace at last? If so, her disillusionment must have been painful indeed. I sensed that her initial loathing of Australia was so profound that she could find no beauty in it anywhere. Often they came with us on one of our boring Sunday drives – a fifties' form of torture for children, who fought in the back seat of the Holden, got car-sick and vomited on the side of the road.

'Isn't this beautiful?' my mother said hopefully, encouragingly, sweeping her arm to indicate the primeval emptiness which folded away in every direction.

'Oo aye,' said Bunty, her lips compressing. It was not beautiful and it was not Scotland. Through her eyes I glimpsed what the first settlers must have seen, and understood how much they must have ached.

I do not know Ted's story, but I gleaned from the way my parents spoke that his sufferings during the war would have been inconceivable to people like us. And here he was, in the back blocks of nowhere, burning himself up – aware, no doubt, behind his shy smile, of the indifferent, faintly contemptuous attitude towards people like himself of the nation to which he now belonged.

Our neighbours on the other side were dairy farmers, and it wasn't just the threat of their crazed Jersey bull which made my mother caution us against crossing the boundary fence. There was an aura of mystery surrounding them, and I did not understand until later that it emanated from the kind of squalor abject poverty can produce. There must have been fourteen children, few of whom ever went to school. My father often grumbled that their fences needed mending, and when they came through our property they left the gates open and stole guavas. He shook his head ruefully, and pronounced them 'no-hopers'.

While the academic education provided by Mooloolah state school was virtually non-existent, there is one thing which must be said in its favour. Everyone, from upper-crust to hill-billy, had a turn at being the victim. Colour, race or class had little to do with the pecking order. Everyone was treated equally badly; everyone had at least one quality for which he or she could be teased, bullied and persecuted. A funny nose, a funny name, it didn't matter much. It was there in the playground that young Australians, old and new,

*Left: A lively Saturday night square dance
in a village hall – local entertainment such
as this was undermined by the advent of
television*
*Below: The post office and store was the
centre of local activity and gossip for many
bush-dwellers*

Opposite: 'I stood on the beach, raised my eighteen-year-old arms towards the apartment blocks rising like honeycomb out of the cliffs, and proclaimed Sydney mine, all mine.'

learned the art of sniffing out and snuffing out difference of any kind, and excellence in any form – except, perhaps, brute strength; where baby poppies learned to hack each other off at the stem as soon as they looked like growing tall. Schooldays were the incubation period for a national lack of self-esteem. To be 'up oneself', to be 'too big for one's boots', to be a 'smart Alec' – these were the commonest forms of abuse.

In the population at large this cultural inferiority complex, this surly defensiveness, manifested itself in an obsession with assimilation. Immigrants were tolerated if they ate our kind of food, believed in our values and learned how to cop insults with a self-deprecating grin. Nino Culotta, an Italian immigrant who wrote a book called *They're a Weird Mob*, was both comic and forgiving in his description of the mutual puzzlement of old Aussie and new. The book was very popular in the late fifties: white Australia liked the image of itself that he created. But what the book revealed was the fact that Australia was willing to accept immigrants only to the same degree to which the immigrants were willing to adapt, to assimilate. When 'otherness' could not, or would not, be disguised, when the skin was too black or the eyes too slanted, the more brutal forms of racism appeared. But every cloud has a silver lining. It was in the playground that little Australians also developed their inbuilt bullshit detectors, their lack of undue reverence, their mistrust of elitism and their laconic, ironic, dry-creek-bed, self-flagellating wit. Australians will be the first to send themselves up, as if, expecting to be laughed at by the world, they can maintain a certain dignity by laughing at themselves first.

Gypsies have always frightened sedentary populations with their 'otherness', and it was no different in Mooloolah. They parked their wagons and grazed their horses on the field near the railway station, sharpened a few knives and scissors, then passed on. I don't think anyone ever said, 'Don't go near the tinkers' camp', but I somehow absorbed – from my family, from my teachers – that it was not a wise thing to do. I deeply regret not having followed the dictates of my own curiosity. By the late fifties they had disappeared. Whether they withdrew from Australia, or whether they were gradually absorbed into the dominant culture, I do not know. In either case, the great Australian drive towards homogeneity had won out.

That the great drive did not succeed, after two hundred years of sustained effort, in turning Aborigines into white men has everything to do with the resilience of Aboriginal culture, of which I had no inkling in my youth. Perhaps if there had been any Aboriginal families left in the area I might have received information different from that provided by the social studies books at school, which portrayed Aboriginal people as ignorant, barbaric creatures with dirty habits, inferior in all mental and spiritual processes to the white man, which was why their demise was inevitable. (This description is still being taught in primary schools, at least in Queensland.) But there were no Aborigines here. The survivors of disease and war had been rounded up and sent to government

Queensland's Gold Coast, the haunt of 'zinc-nosed surfers and life-savers'

Left: 'Dinner in a closed up pigeon-box house ... while cricket commentary droned out of the radio and pigeons cooed in the neat back yards of an infinite suburbia, and nothing dangerous was said'
Right: A farmhouse in Queensland

*Right and far right:
'Many people have
asked me why did I . . .
work for two years to
get myself some
camels, then drag them
across half a continent
full of emptiness and
flies.' The attraction
of Australia's 'red
heart' is one of the
land's many paradoxes*

*Below: Aboriginal
stockmen in northern
Queensland*

settlements which were, and still are, concentration camps – out of sight, out of mind.

'Poor old Abos, they were a fine people,' said my father with genuine sadness.

> Eenie, meenie, minie, mo,
> Catch a nigger by the toe,
> If he screams, let him go,
> Eenie, meenie, minie, mo

sang the children at school.

'Tidy this room please, children. It looks like a blacks' camp,' said the teacher.

Cultivating a tolerance of difference was not one of Mooloolah's gifts to its children, but it was a wonderful place for the free development of the imagination. Without the restrictions of television and masses of toys, my sister and I constructed worlds out of dirt, sticks and pebbles and populated the countryside with fabulous creations. We were bursting with the vitality produced by a diet which was the best the earth could offer – fresh fish, every kind of fruit and vegetable, home-baked bread, milk straight from the udder, home-grown mutton. To those not initiated into the secrets of our games, Mooloolah might have seemed a dull place. To us, it was paradise.

I am still struck by the physicality and self-reliance of Australian children. They are more often than not riding surfboards by the time they are six, and producing skin cancers by the time they are twenty. With all that energy and weather, who could bear to be inside studying, or reading books, or practising the piano, or learning how to make polite conversation with grown-ups? My mother worried, therefore, that we might grow up unrefined and without accomplishments. Once a fortnight we were taken to Nambour, our nearest town, to sit at the piano and have pennies placed on our wrists by nuns with rulers in their hands. Every three weeks three books would arrive by post, which I would have to pretend to read. One day my mother caught me out.

'Did you enjoy your book about Mozart?'

'Oh, yesss.'

'All right, then. What was his first name?' After a few moments of silence she pointed to the title spread right across the cover – *Wolfgang Amadeus Mozart*.

'I just forgot,' I said, and got whacked with the book.

'If she's so anxious for me to read,' I thought, 'how come she locks some books in a cupboard? *Lady Chatterley's Lover*, for example, and *Ulysses*.'

She battled, too, to bring an appreciation of the higher things to the culturally deprived people of Mooloolah. Under her guiding hand, night life flourished in the School of Arts Hall. Theatrical events were staged in which I featured heavily. In my time I have been both a Wattle Fairy (I was so *embarrassed* by those yellow bloomers) and Mary, Mother of Jesus. I have sung 'Life is Great in the Sunshine State' to audiences who cheered my high C. The older kids got

Opposite: 'I sat outside under the grapevines and jasmine . . . listening to ocean noises, wondering why the hell I ever went away.' Sun, sea and surfing are some of the more physical pleasures that draw expatriates back to their native Australia

to sing 'Tan Shoes and Pink Shoelaces', which I thought was rather unfair, but I took what parts were offered.

She scoured the district for women who could play the piano. While the men scattered Pops Dancing Dust on the floor the ladies took turns on stage, thumping out waltz tunes all in the same key. Men scrubbed up, slicked their hair down with Californian Poppy, and donned broad-lapelled suits if they had them, clean shirts and khaki trousers if they didn't. Women wore mid-length dresses with gathered skirts, and when they stepped out for the Pride of Erin or the progressive barn dance the men placed a handkerchief chivalrously against their partners' backs so as not to mark the pretty frocks. Alcohol was forbidden. Wooden seats borrowed from the school lined the four sides of the hall, one of which opened on to an annexe where tea in glass cups would be served at supper, along with the sandwiches, scones, pikelets and lamingtons that the ladies had made that afternoon. At 10 p.m. the dancing would end and supper would be called – children first, then adults. And while the adults were sipping their tea with little fingers outstretched, and yarning about weather and falling pineapple prices, the children would drag each other, horse-and-cart style, from one end of the slippery floor to the other.

But the excesses of Saturday night had to be paid for by the sobriety of Sunday mornings. Oh, how I loathed Sunday school. Oh, how I despaired of the fortnightly visits of the preacher, who maundered on and on and on like a blowfly, while our scalps itched under our white panama hats, and our knickers prickled under pastel nylon frocks, and our palms perspired on to our plastic purses which contained nothing other than a freshly ironed hanky and sixpence for the collection plate. Could there have been a worse torment than sitting in the heat, watching my dad embarrass my mum by dropping off in the pew and snoring, until the tattered little congregation burst forth with 'Bringing in the Sheep'?

Yes. Our increasingly frequent visits to the city. Now when I say 'city' I really mean large, sprawling country town, whose most exciting shops were Myer's Emporium and Dalgety's Stock and Station Agents. Brisbane was a dreamy, languid place, a town of never-ending Sundays. Long, exhausting journeys on the train ended in a dose of cod liver oil from my grandmother who would be waiting, spoon poised, at the other end. After recovering from that there would be baked dinner in a closed up pigeon-box house, whose windows would be bolted and curtains drawn against the vulgarity of Australia's weather. Sweat dribbled silently on to the starched linen napkins which we were allowed to tuck into our lace collars, while cricket commentary droned out of the radio and pigeons cooed in the neat back yards of an infinite suburbia, and nothing dangerous was said.

I think these visits were most difficult for my father, who, when released from the cramped confines of the interior, would look out over the rapidly spreading suburbs of fibro and weatherboard and reminisce about the time when all this had been a paper-bark swamp: 'I used to hunt black duck here when I was a boy. The creeks were fresh and clean, full of fish. There used to be white sandbanks in the Brisbane River. But you've got to have progress.'

It would be many years before Anglo-Saxon Australians opened their architecture and their eyes to the wonders which surrounded them. The Italians and Greeks, and later on the Asians, were partly to thank for that. Small windows and rose trellises gave way to grapevined patios and skylights. Houses which had originally been built to face the street were reorganised to open on to ocean views or parks. But, at the time, being closed in was considered the English and therefore the correct way to go about things. Even Rowe's Café, which was 'it' for sophistication in Brisbane, did not allow air to penetrate its darkened rooms. The furniture was black, the tablecloths pure white. Cucumber sandwiches and Devonshire teas were served by waiters who did not smile.

We were unprepared, therefore, for our first visit to a 'fair dinkum' city – Sydney. My mother had wealthy relatives there, who had made their money out of refrigerators. They lived in a modest mansion down by the harbour where they had a swimming pool and a real tiger rug. They drank sweet, bubbly Porphyry Pearl wine rather than beer. They took us for rides in their long black car, and introduced us to Culture. My mother never forgave my father for eating peanuts and clacking his dentures through a performance of *Swan Lake*.

We decided to be daredevils and try out some foreign food in one of the first Italian restaurants in Sydney. My mother's face twisted into an attitude of deep revulsion as she twizzled her fork in the spaghetti. 'It's got *garlic* in it!' she cried. But other palates were being seduced by these new tastes. Take-away chicken chow mein was competing with greasy fish and chips. Spices were introduced to home cooking. However, in less sophisticated areas of Australia I have heard it said – and recently – that only dagos eat garlic, and only poofters go in for sour cream.

The decade was coming to an end, and so were my sister's utopian days. Puberty struck, and whatever else may be said in Mooloolah's favour its teenage social life was not exactly swinging. My pain at her disappearance into adulthood and boarding school was somewhat alleviated by the advent of television. When we made our fortnightly visits to Nambour these days we would see knots of people crowded around shop windows, their blank faces flickering in the spectral lights of the magic box. When the stationmaster bought a set we began having social evenings at his house, during which we greatly admired the twenty-six-inch screen sitting inside a rosewood veneer cabinet with legs, and sang along with the advertising jingles. The pressure on my father was enormous, and at last he caved in.

The modern era moved into our lounge room and set about destroying conversation, sing-songs around the piano and our addiction to radio. Previously, our best outing had been going to the Eudlo cinema of a Friday night. (The cinema was a converted School of Arts Hall.) We would pack the utility truck with blankets and thermoses of coffee and head off into the twilight. On the way home I would sleep in the back, under the stars, while my dad swerved to avoid marsupials along twelve miles of gravel road. He had to get into low gear to negotiate the 'pinch', a steep hill where bushrangers had once held up Cobb and Co. coaches. The 'pinch' often held up our 'ute'.

But now our Eudlo adventures were abandoned, along with my timeless afternoons. No longer did I hang around the store with Jennifer Garbutt and Susan Turner, swapping penny lollies after school. No longer did I collect botanical specimens and dead insects for my scrapbooks, or spend hours on the swing, composing symphonies and poems. No longer did I race down to the paddocks to 'help' my father with the shearing/dipping/drenching/milking, and to listen to him talk about infinity and other great matters. Now it was home lickety-split to grab a Vegemite sandwich and join in the singing of 'M-I-C-K-E-Y M-O-U-S-E' with a pair of black plastic ears stuck on my head.

In 1959 my mother became ill and we decided to join the ever-increasing surge of people leaving country areas for the towns and cities, where doctors and jobs were prevalent. Perhaps the decision had as much to do with our failure to make money out of Malabah, but whatever the cause the move marked a profound change for all of us. My father entered an uneasy retirement; my mother, a deep depression. And I'm sure my own blanking out of the early sixties had much to do with massive culture shock.

With the sale of Malabah my father had made his last financial blunder. Not too many years later our Mooloolah neighbours would cash in on the land boom and sell their dairy farms to coastal developers for fabulous sums. Later still the hippies would arrive, fresh from the revelations of the Asian trail and with enough wealth behind them to choose poverty as a way of life. They built ashrams and geodesic domes and planted dope where once impoverished dirt-farmers had scratched to earn a living. I have not been back, but I hear that Malabah's sheep have been replaced by quickly replicating brick veneer houses with exposed aggregate gardens and mock Roman columns. And the wild beaches and the wallum country behind them are now crowded with high-rise developments. Paradise lost.

If life in the country in the fifties meant isolation, in the suburbs it meant loneliness. Here we were, surrounded by an ocean of houses, but where was the community? What would take the place of the dances in the School of Arts Hall, or the kinds of bonds created between men and women when they set out together with their hessian sacks to fight the bush fires? In the kitchen we had an electric stove, a fridge and a Mix-master. We had a vacuum cleaner and a floor polisher. On Sundays it was the whirring of Victa lawn-mowers which woke us up rather than the chorus of songbirds. We had a television which cost £250, and we had more time than we had ever had before in which to do

nothing. Which is mostly what we did.

My father twiddled his thumbs and dug the garden. Some days he went
fishing for flat-head in the estuary, but it wasn't much fun alone. My mother
stared out of windows a great deal and took handfuls of Bex powders (an
analgesic which was the forerunner of Valium) with tonic water. We all spent
a lot of time watching *I Love Lucy*, *Perry Mason*, *The Cisco Kid*, *77 Sunset Strip*,
Liberace and *Pick-a-Box* on television. My sister, five years older and more
worldly than me, watched *Bandstand* and *Six O'clock Rock* during her infrequent
visits home from school. I spent most of my time strolling across the golf course
which bordered our house, worrying about just what it was that went on
behind the lavatories at my new school. In Mooloolah there had been thirty
pupils in the whole school. Now there were thirty in my class. Thirty children
who rode bicycles rather than horses and knew all about sex.

By now Australia's infatuation with America was manifesting itself in an
obsession not only with American fast food, American films, American music
and American comics, but also with American politics. When Kennedy was
shot, many children my age wept for the leader of the world, but would not
have been able to name their own Prime Minister. Along with the washing
machines and crop-dusters came the tackier kinds of American artefacts, which
most Australians accepted uncritically. We even contributed our own inven-
tiveness to the visual blight which was taking over the towns and suburbs, of
which coloured plastic bunting and brick veneer are only two examples. But
generally speaking, our own innovations were not backed. An Australian had
discovered refrigeration back in 1850, but imported ice from America was
considered of superior quality. So it was with computers and transistors. Our
technology was well ahead, but it was decided that Australia was too small to
develop its own manufacturing industries. Perhaps it was a lack of confidence
which prevented us from competing with the rest of the world. Whatever the
cause, the decision to base our economy on primary industries has led to the
present dire economic situation, in which the Australian dollar is laughingly
referred to as the Pacific peso.

I read somewhere recently an argument for suburban living. 'It reconciles
access to work and city with private, adaptable, self-expressive living space at
home. Plenty of adults love that living space, and subdivide it ingeniously. For
children it really has no rivals.' I suspect that the man who wrote it had not
spent time in places like Redcliffe. Perhaps my loneliness would have been
assuaged if I'd joined in the throbbing social life centred around Redcliffe's
cinema. But my mother was over-protective and, besides, the cinema was the
meeting ground for those purveyors of decadent values, the Bodgies and
Widgies, who offended social *mores* by going in for unconventional fashion –
stovepipe trousers did not conceal Presley purple socks. The Widgies lolled on
the backs of their Bodgies' bikes, jingling razor-blade bracelets.

To my parents, these rebels without a cause were a symbol of everything
that was going wrong in the world – the traditional values of hard work,

puritanism and thrift, developed through first the Depression and then the war, were being mocked and undermined. Every Saturday night teams of these youngsters would ride their bikes up from Brisbane to hang around outside hamburger shops, terrorising the sleepy residents of the backwater with the insolent way they sucked on their milk-shakes.

My father believed that these 'juvenile delinquents' should be drafted into the army to make men of them. As for me, I was both frightened and fascinated. They were like butterflies with poisonous stings and they seemed to be having more fun than I was. Sometimes I was allowed to go to the Saturday matinée at the cinema with the older boys from next door. They had an F.J. Holden, they were reliable, and they didn't mind having a little kid along. There I discovered that the Bodgies' pranks were pretty tame – lots of whistling, lots of necking with Widgies up the back, lots of Jaffas being rolled down under the seats, but nothing dangerous. Alas, these Saturday outings were stopped when a more serious faction who mixed hard liquor with their milk-shakes came into the theatre and ran up and down the aisles slashing the seats with flick-knives.

By the time my sister left school she was well on the way to becoming a wild one, but of the beatnik variety. My mother admonished her to buy cotton frocks and sensible shoes; she went in for black sloppy joes, white lipstick and Intimate perfume. She gave me cigarettes to smoke in the toilet when I was eleven, and hinted that there was life beyond Redcliffe. She was standing on the wrong side of the generation gap and I ached to join her, but I had my four-year stretch in boarding school to live through before I could take the leap.

Australia is often described as a classless society. The squattocracy was the closest to an upper class that it ever produced, but even the squatters were forced by isolation and economic circumstances to be more intimate with and dependent upon their workers than were their British forbears. In the middle of the last century, the gold rush created a new bourgeoisie who could be heard to say, as they lit their cigars with £10 notes, that they were the aristocracy now. Then as now, if you had money you had class. One of the ways of buying class in Australia is to pay out exorbitant sums on a private education for your children. In my day these schools were poor, indeed ludicrous, replicas of English public schools. Their emphasis was not upon education but upon producing snobs who were fit to marry other snobs. To go out with a boy from a state school was enough to make you a social outcast. To admit that your family voted Labor was to give away a sordid working-class background. The very word 'Labor' had a nasty ring: it conjured up visions of coarse, sweaty men who would only wear white collars on Sundays.

We were seldom allowed to watch television at school, and never allowed to read newspapers. It was hinted, in our final year, that universities were places where doctors and lawyers went, but the prospective wives of doctors and

Opposite: When British fashion model Jean Shrimpton wore an albeit demure mini-skirt to the Melbourne Cup in 1965, Australian matrons were either amused or scandalised

lawyers did not. All sorts of social causes were claiming the youth of the country (40 per cent of the population was now under twenty-one), but the girls of St Margaret's School remained oblivious. The first sounds of mass radicalism on the streets did not penetrate the high walls of the grounds. We heard no revolutionary messages in the music we listened to. Socialism was regarded as a kind of social leprosy. When Lyndon Baines Johnson visited Australia in 1966 our school organised a parade to line the streets and wave, just as we had waved to the Queen in previous years. But the canon who took chapel that day stretched the service out with a sermon concerning the evils of war, thereby depriving us of the possibility of going 'all the way with L.B.J.'. 'That canon must be some kind of Pinko,' we all agreed.

My unfocused rebellion led me to skip classes and spend most of my time in the music rooms, thumping out passionate rhapsodies and practising for the day when I would fulfil my mother's dream and become a famous concert pianist. Consequently I received a scholarship to the Conservatorium of Music but missed out on one to the University. Music was, in fact, our one legitimised contact with the world outside. Every Saturday night we were allowed to play our records and practise jiving, twisting and surfie-stomping with each other, while the nuns' heads bobbed up and down to the beat of 'Bombora', 'Roll Over Beethoven' and 'Blue Gene'. There was much debate over which of the Beatles was the most desirable, and whether the Rolling Stones could ever match up. Another topic of conversation was how minuscule you could make your bikini and still stay within beach regulations. On one of my few holidays up the coast with a schoolfriend, my one-piece costume guaranteed wallflower status on the sands. Zinc-nosed surfies and life-savers just passed me by. In 1962 Tania Verstak, the daughter of White Russian immigrants, won Miss Australia, Miss International and all our hearts by being so unfailingly nice. Her adoring public referred to her as 'an adopted daughter' who had made the most of her 'fair go'. A mere three years later Jean Shrimpton would shatter these ideals of womanhood by wearing, to the Melbourne Cup, a mini-skirt a daring four inches above the knee. Wholesomeness was on the way out.

When Menzies introduced decimal currency there were rhymes and jingles to help us sort out pennies from cents. No doubt the confusion disguised the fact that buying power at the tuck-shop was less with the pretty new coins. He retired that same year, and was followed by a quick succession of Prime Ministers who dithered helplessly in the face of an urge for social change. After a year in power Harold Holt vanished into the surf at Portsea, and shortly after that I vanished from the school arena. Rumours of Chinese submarines and frogmen assassins excited the imagination of Australians far more than the most likely explanation of his demise – that he had been caught in a rip tide.

Like any released prisoner I had to learn what had happened to the world while I was 'inside'. I set about discovering the sixties. The country was wealthier than it had ever been, thanks to a mining boom reminiscent of the old gold rush days. But despite this Australia was experiencing an upheaval such as it had never had before: it was being torn apart. There were many issues over which dissension arose, but the main one was, of course, the conscription of young, voteless Australian men, by ballot, to fight in Vietnam. A hundred thousand moratorium marchers stopped the traffic in major cities. This sort of thing might happen in other countries, but surely not in dear old sleepy Australia! The Labor opposition leader, Arthur Calwell, had stated: 'There are great issues that demand that every politician should stand up for the truth as he sees it and take the consequences.' One consequence of his anti-Vietnam stance was that Labor would remain out of power until the Liberal-Country Party was let down by Nixon, until public opinion changed, until 1972 when Gough Whitlam accelerated the troop withdrawal initiated by McMahon a few months earlier.

This was the state of the world I entered, and I joined the flood of demonstrators like a duck taking to water. I gave up my scholarship to the Conservatorium (the students there seemed to be fiddling while Rome burned) and began hanging around at Queensland University, arguably the most radicalised campus in Australia. I got a job there which allowed me to attend courses free of charge at night – although I have to admit that academic education was not what I was after. I wanted to *live*.

The particular vociferousness of student unrest in my home state was due to the outlandish conservatism of the state government. I think we described it as 'fascist' at the time. Certainly there were more than enough repressive laws against which to fight. Queensland had already distinguished itself by being the first state to arrest anti-conscription marchers – setting a long tradition of proscribing any form of dissent. When widespread demonstrations were expected on the arrival in Brisbane of the Springbok rugby union team in 1971, a state of emergency was announced, giving the Queensland government unlimited power throughout the state for one month. Ironically, it had been a Labor government which had invested the Cabinet with such powers, just as it had been a Labor government which instigated the gerrymandering which would later be used so skilfully by the Conservatives to stay in power.

The *bête noire* of Queensland students was the Premier, Johannes Bjelke Petersen, a fundamentalist Christian, passionately anti-socialist and committed to unfettered development, a man who was against 'Communists, strikes, rabble-rousers, Communist-manipulated demonstrations, the welfare state, the dole, drugs, long-hairs, bludgers'. Sir Joh was, and still is, treated as something of a joke by chauvinistic southerners, who refer to Queensland as 'The Deep North'. They heap ridicule upon him but this only endears him further to his supporters. A long history of underdevelopment in the state has given rise to a population who feel a great deal of sympathy for a leader who claims to 'stand up for Queensland'.

I have thought many things about the Premier, but unlike many of my peers

Above: Anti-Vietnam demonstrators from Sydney University cause Menzies to throw up his hands in mock horror

Left: Two Australian privates on a Christmas shopping spree by pedicab

I have never thought him a fool. He is one of the most ruthless and clever political leaders in the country, and time and again has shown himself to be more than a match for enemy politicians. He has championed states rights and tested the limits of Australian federalism; he has rarely lost a confrontation with Canberra; he has God and the multinationals on his side.

The Queenslanders who suffer most from his policies are the Aborigines. The state has the largest population of blacks in Australia and the most draconian laws governing them. Eleven articles of the United Nations Universal Declaration of Human Rights are broken by these laws. The assimilation policy remains unchanged; land rights are out of the question. Some settlements have the highest incidence of violent crime anywhere in the world; standards of health are shamefully low. When representatives of the World Council of Churches visited Australia to compile a report on discrimination and injustice, the Premier would not allow his officials to meet with them. When a team of medical people went to black communities throughout Australia in an attempt to eradicate trachoma, an eye disease which afflicts – often blinds – one in four Aboriginal people, Bjelke sent them packing because they were 'encouraging Aborigines to vote'. When a referendum was passed in 1967, giving the federal government powers to legislate for Aborigines over the states, everyone thought that things would improve. But Bjelke has continually and successfully blocked any attempts at 'interference'.

His version of the Protestant work ethic ensured a place for him in my father's heart, even if his religious beliefs did not. Political arguments were beginning to develop between us, which were only exacerbated by my father's infrequent visits to the 'commune' where I now lived. No more than a senescent but still glorious house, which I shared with several other people attached to the university, it was one of the happiest, most supportive households I have ever had the pleasure to live in – but my father thought it was a snake-pit. Perhaps he was even a little jealous of the spirit of comradeship which bound young people together in those days. Having spurned the nuclear family unit, we immediately set about creating family relationships with each other, some of which would survive changing beliefs, different lifestyles and demographic shifts on a global scale.

When my father visited, young men covered in unkempt hair did not get up to shake his hand. Women in army fatigues or see-through kaftans revealed bra-less chests. Posters of Lenin glowered down at two weeks' worth of washing up stacked in the kitchen sink. But what he found really intolerable were the new words which peppered our language – words like 'fuck', 'fuckin'' or 'fucked', as in 'Most people over forty are fucked.' My dear old dad was deaf to the answers that were blowing in the wind, and all he could see was the insufferable arrogance of a spoilt generation.

My visits to him were only slightly more satisfactory. 'Gawd, Rob,' he would say, as soon as I met him at the door, 'haven't you got a nice dress to wear?' Tersely I would assure him that I liked wearing men's bowling trousers, a jumper with holes in it, red patent leather boots and a beret. Within five minutes we would be arguing. I would accuse him of being an old reactionary, who didn't know what he was talking about. He would accuse me of being a silly young twerp, who didn't know what she was talking about. We were both right.

The one issue which we could discuss without stomping off in mutual incomprehension was conservation. Queensland is endowed with rain forest, desert, the Great Barrier Reef, dream beaches and some unique islands off the coast near Brisbane which are made entirely of sand. Previously, most mining in the state had taken place out in the 'donga', where no one except the Aborigines who lived there cared too much about the environmental damage it was causing. But when the sand miners almost devastated Fraser Island in their search for rutile, even my father thought about changing his vote. It was only a momentary wavering, however, and his dedication to progress won out in the end. The Fraser Island dispute was one of the few that Bjelke's forces lost to the conservationists, although it would take ten years for the federal government to refuse to give export approvals to the company, before the Australian Heritage Commission was established and listed Fraser Island under the National Estate.

Just as our Premier was urging Australians to

Go north young man, to the frontier where the future for growth is so great that it staggers the imagination . . . where the spirit of adventure will triumph over adversity given the right economic environment, the courage of our people and the pioneering zeal of our great companies . . . where there are endless opportunities for people with enterprise and initiative and not afraid of hard work. Where our destiny is to populate, occupy and exploit our opportunities as never before. . . .

I was deciding to take my enterprise and initiative south, to Sydney. I am sure that, had Bjelke known of my departure, he would not have been sorry. I was leaving room for the older, richer folk who were heading into the Sunshine State to escape death duties.

The overnight train journey from Brisbane to Sydney takes sixteen hours – plenty of time in which to wonder whether you are doing the right thing. The design of the seats renders comfort impossible in any position. Sleep is out of the question. While I was confident that I possessed the three passports to success – a sleeping bag, a packet of oral contraceptives and several addresses – Sydney, I knew, would be no pushover. It would be very racy and very *big*.

I arrived early on a Sunday morning to find it very deserted. The only sign of life was a newspaper whipping down the gutter and a seedy little man in a

Above: Throughout the sixties and seventies opposition to Australian involvement in Vietnam grew steadily louder

Opposite above: Sydney in the days of flower-power. Oxford Street market, Paddington
Opposite below: The older generation was baffled by the sudden emergence of hippy culture

greatcoat leaning into a corner. Where was the high life, the extravagant bohemianism, the glittering sophistication? My disappointment turned to anxiety when the seedy little man started following me down the street, muttering lewd things and taking sips from a bottle of meths. The miserable dawn had the smell of sea kelp and stale beer in it. Half an hour later I realised that I had taken the wrong direction and was lost somewhere in the semi-slum area of Ultimo, an inner-city suburb which would have to wait years for its turn at gentrification. Eventually I took a taxi. I will always remember that drive as a kind of surfacing from the cold ocean depths up into the light. Sydney revealed its beauty coquettishly, lifting its grey, obscuring veils with each passing mile. By the time I reached Bondi I was dazzled by it, converted to it, thoroughly seduced by it.

Previously I had thought of cities simply as places where more people lived and therefore more things happened. Social cesspits. I had never associated physical beauty with them – that belonged exclusively to the country. I stood on the beach, raised my eighteen-year-old arms towards the apartment blocks rising like honeycomb out of the cliffs, and proclaimed Sydney mine, all mine. I never come home to it now without experiencing that same lift in spirit and quickening of pulse.

My detailed exploration of this tremendously varied city began with King's Cross, which had once been the red-lit centre of bohemian life and was now being invaded by sleazy strip-joints, tattoo shops and night-clubs providing entertainment for Vietnam soldiers on R. and R. When the war was over, the sleaze remained – fertile ground for heroin addiction and child prostitution, the scourge of suburban family life. These days, eleven-year-old runaways trade cheap sex for expensive drugs. Just down from the Cross was a lovely street graced with plane trees and elegant Victorian houses. From there I walked down a flight of a hundred or so sandstone steps until I reached the harbour and Wooloomooloo, or the 'Loo as locals prefer to call it. Both Victoria Street and the 'Loo were destined for fame, as front lines in the battle between developers and residents.

All over the city, buttresses and ridges of warm golden rock rose up unexpectedly. Little Moreton Bay figs clung to the walls of old buildings built of the same glowing sandstone. In the commercial centre, parks and gardens flanked giant monoliths around which blew sea breezes and city grit. The harbour itself, indented with tiny coves of white sand, opened to the ocean at the Heads – a mile-wide entrance on either side of which stood vertical cliffs two hundred feet high. Rows of terraced houses with red-tiled roofs, built a century ago, nestled next to precipices or lined up along hillsides overlooking the sea. Everywhere there were restaurants. Excellent restaurants. The recent immigrants, bless their hearts, gave Australia many gifts, but the greatest of these was food.

Even without the addresses I had, I would soon have made friends: the counter-culture was very generous towards people of like mind. I could have walked up to any hippie in the park, or tapped on the shoulder of any of the thousands of demonstrators, and been fairly certain that I could find a floor to sleep on, if not a bed. After a lot of shoulder tapping I found my way to the fringes of the Sydney Push – a loose confederation of intellectuals, artists, renegades, radicals, eccentrics, ex-cons, Commies, misfits and bon vivants of all types, ages and backgrounds.

Previously, Australia's artists had tended to flee from the land of Sunday afternoons. Now they were more often than not staying home, or even coming back to sell their work to a population whose cultural appetites, so long fed on overseas produce, were beginning to find Australian flavours equally to their taste. Galleries popped up overnight like mushrooms. Germaine Greer published *The Female Eunuch*, Dennis Altman published *Homosexuality*. The Balmain poets gave readings in the pubs during breaks in the jazz music which spilled into the streets. Patrick White won the Nobel Prize for Literature. The Nimrod Theatre opened and put on plays by David Williamson and Alex Buzo. *Oz* had died, but its satirical spirit lived on. The *Nation Review* was Australia's *Village Voice* – a display case for a new kind of journalism and for the genius of two young cartoonists – Michael Leunig and Patrick Cook.

If you couldn't afford tickets to the Opera House, you had the chance of taking your culture in comfort during a free concert in Hyde Park, where a crowd of several thousand gathered under a big yellow moon, sipping Chablis and slurping oysters and drowning in Joan Sutherland's decibels. If opera wasn't to your taste you could go to the same park the following day and listen to rock bands, or to the Yellow House, where Sydney's young Van Goghs displayed their talents and 'happenings' happened. Besides all that there was Mediterranean weather and scores of beaches on which to enjoy it – little private beaches snuggled into corners of the harbour and big public beaches between cliffs pounded by the Pacific.

The most popular of these was, and still is, Bondi. It is here that Australia displays itself in all its naked glory. Or almost naked. On the weekends, people flock to it like terns. Greeks, Italians, Asians, Aborigines and Europeans stroll along the paths skirting the headlands, or line up next to each other on the sand like so many sausages. Gorgeous models wearing nothing but gold kid-leather G-strings sip Moët next to suburban working-class families with eskies full of Foster's and watermelon. Greek grannies dressed all in black watch great-grandchildren playing footie or frisbee by the water's edge. In the early eighties, a local sports commentator who wanted to see the law changed regarding topless bathing – which many of Sydney's beaches allow – said that he did not like having other people's genitals thrust in his face. But most beach-goers, it seems, are not offended by the uninhibited display of flesh. Indeed, they seem to be having too good a time to notice.

Having a good time, I was soon to discover, was what Sydney was all about.

Where Brisbane had been dour and serious and full of grim concern, Sydney was Dionysian, vital and full of hedonism. Having a good time was a political act. A cornucopia of drugs helped, or in many cases hindered, the process. Vitamin B shots for alcoholic poisoning were popular. It was as if I had arrived at a never-ending party, to which the only entry requirement was a capacity for outrage or outrageousness. Perhaps my inability to remember details of my three years there is because I am still suffering from the hangover.

There were casualties, of course, and I would be the last to say that it was an ideal time to be growing up. But the one great gift from the late sixties and early seventies to those of us who were formed by it, who survived it, was the sense that anything was possible. A diverse range of political and social ginger groups raised the level of debate concerning which direction the country should be taking. They confronted a previously uncaring population with the injustices and bigotries inherent in Australian society, gradually preparing the ground for a change of government. Feminism raised its head, looked around and growled. While some members of the Push were defensive about this, and could be heard to say things like 'What are you growling at us for, we were the first to let you into our pubs', a spiky camaraderie between the sexes continued to exist.

The early seventies also gave its generation a lot of time in which to contemplate its navel. The counter-culture was dividing up, amoeba-like, and the main split was between the seekers after spiritual truth and the seekers after social justice. The hippie trail was a one-way trade route along which Buddhism in all its forms, sarongs, batik, shell wind-chimes and hepatitis were imported from Asia. In previous generations Australia had felt itself to be inferior to Europe and superior to Asia. Now the country's youth had discovered Asia and was turning its back contemptuously on Europe. The I Ching replaced the Bible, and in just about every bookcase Alan Watts and Dr Suzuki sat next to Hermann Hesse and R. D. Laing. They all stank of patchouli oil. Eastern mysticism continued to do very well in Australia long after it became passé in other western countries, and Sydney streets still contain almost as many saffron robes as Bangkok. Perhaps there is something in the twisted, freakish landscape which encourages mystical contemplation. There is nothing quite as other-worldly, nothing quite as queer to the eye as the Australian bush.

Adherents to the alternative lifestyle found ideal settings in the lush forests and along the beaches further north. The farmers who lived there were not terribly happy about this sudden invasion of naked aliens who left gates open and shat behind bushes or, worse still, in the mobile communal toilets which had been brought for the thousands who attended the Nimbin festival – Australia's very own Woodstock. After it was all over and the police, who'd arrived like cockroaches to leftovers, had gone home, groups of 'alternates' banded together to buy land, and set up communes where they could pluck psychedelic mushrooms from cowpats and put street politics behind them. Earth mothers popped out babies while their men attacked the impenetrable thickets of lantana with machetes, causing about as much damage to the weed as my father's axe had caused the brigalow.

The farmers simply could not understand how these people could throw away all the opportunities to which they, the farmers, aspired and choose to live in converted cow-bails. As if this wilful lowering of standards weren't enough, the newcomers were against forestry logging – the only industry in the area providing jobs. Gradually the drop-outs realised, just as the red-necks had before them, that ideologically pure farming did not pay. The siege mentality between the two communities began to ease when farm machinery replaced machetes on the communes and when artists and craftsmen opened shops and brought money to the area.

There were population shifts within the city too. I lived in many suburbs during my time in Sydney, and remained in each one of them until wealthier folk, armed with cans of white paint, arrived in their new Mini-Mokes, pushing rents up and me out. Gentrification of the inner city was forcing working-class people to shift twenty miles out into the western suburbs, which lacked the amenities and resources of richer areas.

While the middle classes were anxious to pretty up and preserve the workers' cottages they had just bought, developers were anxious to pull them down; in this they had the support of city councillors, some of whom were not above accepting a bribe. Sydney had grown convulsively after the war, and no coherent urban planning policy had ever been implemented. The beautiful old city was to be torn down to make way for high-rise development; parkland was to be taken over for housing; freeways were to invade the centre like thread-worms; Centennial Park was to be covered by a sporting complex; the Botanical Gardens were to have a vast car park built beneath them. Wooloomooloo and the oldest area of Sydney, the Rocks, were first on the hit list for redevelopment. The 'Loo project called for eighteen high-rise office blocks and luxury hotels on eleven acres of land previously covered in high-density housing. The city council granted approval. The fight was on.

Middle class and working class banded together in a common cause. Local associations, anxious to preserve the aesthetic quality of their choice residential areas, were the forerunners of more politically oriented resident action groups, some of whom joined local councils. Others used more direct forms of protest – they demonstrated, they barricaded themselves into their homes when the bulldozers came, they squatted in houses listed for demolition, they created a lot of fuss and noise, and they called on the support of the Builders' Labourers' Federation, who placed 'green bans' on the multitude of development projects threatening the city. The BLF was a unique union. By withholding labour from various development proposals it saved the parks, the foreshores and many historic buildings and residential areas. It also brought the issues involved to the attention of the public. It has since been torn apart by internal dissension, but it is thanks to its green bans that Sydney escaped so much mindless

Freshening up under a 'bush shower' – primitive but effective

destruction. I had left by the time the most bitter clash between developers and residents raged in Victoria Street. Thugs had been hired from nearby King's Cross to evict squatters, usually brutally. People were hurt, and one woman journalist 'disappeared'. While everyone involved in the Victoria Street battle believed that she had been abducted and murdered by members of the underworld working for the developers, it was another matter to bring it to court.

The end of the early seventies was signalled by creeping inflation and rising unemployment. For the first time since the Depression, Australians found themselves looking for jobs which were not there. It was an inauspicious time for a big-spending government of reform to be seeking office. But public opinion had changed and Labor, led by the dynamic Gough Whitlam, began its campaign under the slogan 'It's time.'

It was also time for me to head back home. Three years in the fast lane had taken their toll. I wanted peace, mangoes and landscape, but most of all I wanted to spend time with my father. Our deep fondness for each other had survived the sixties, and we decided to close the generation gap by going bush and hunting for opals in the desert regions of Queensland's interior.

Up and over the Great Divide, and the first thing I noticed was the smell – a mixture of Mitchell grass and baked earth, redolent of the past. As the miles peeled away the sky became bluer, higher and wider; the road became longer, bumpier and narrower; the road signs of silhouetted kangaroos became rustier and more riddled with bullet holes. Kites turned slowly in the invisible wheels of thermals; flocks of budgerigars, Lincoln parrots and pink and grey galahs rose from the side of the road; rowdy corellas and screeching Major Mitchells the colour of sunsets lifted out of the coolibah trees along the empty creeks; double-bars and spinifex pigeons – clouds of them – skimmed across the top of the grass. The further I journeyed into this bountiful desert, the closer I felt to 'home'.

It was the Australian autumn when I went – April. At night the stars glinted cold and sharp as ice. In the mornings we stamped and blew out mist, waiting for the billy to boil. First light coloured the spinifex heads a pale and delicate gold. The bush seemed so fragile at that hour. Even the bird calls were thin and piping in the cold, clear air as if someone were ringing the lips of a hundred crystal glasses . . . . It was stinking hot by ten.

West of Winton we left the sheep and cattle country behind. No more fences. The opal field was on three million acres of Crown land – country too rugged and parched to support livestock, and as yet unscarred by mineral exploration. The fact that only milky opal was found there, rather than the pin-fire black which so delights overseas buyers, ensured that we would have the place pretty much to ourselves. In fact with our arrival the population rose from two to four.

We set up our camp in hills that have been exposed, cracked, sand-blasted and ground down longer than other hills. Hills that look like decomposing skeletons. The trees gave only an illusion of shade, so we stretched a tarpaulin between two of them. The food we hung in a Coolgardie safe, from the limb of a tree, to protect it from ants and from the marsupial mice who have sweet, pointed faces, a bottle brush on the end of their tails, big, luminous, nocturnal eyes and tiny pouches in which they carry their young. Adorable they may be, but their sweet faces belie avaricious temperaments. They can knock off a damper quick as look at you.

We freshened up under the bush shower rigged from a bough, then set off to make our presence known to our nearest neighbour, whose camp lay thirty miles along a four-wheel-drive track which kept disappearing into creek beds. The two-hour journey brought us to a moonscape of creamy-coloured dust, as bare as sandhills by the sea.

In the distance, Banjo Hunt was a vertical slit in the shimmering wall of heat. As we drew closer, details formed – a ten-gallon hat, bandy legs and then one of those typically gaunt, leathery Australian faces. He must have heard the car approaching a long way off, because the billy was already singing. We didn't want our neighbours to feel crowded out by our presence – people out there like their privacy, their space and their solitary lives. On the other hand, it was bush etiquette to let a neighbour know where you were, so that once a week or thereabouts a surreptitious check could be made to see whether you were still alive.

'G'day,' said Banjo, and squatted by the fire.

'G'day,' said my father and I. The conversation took quite a while to get started. There wasn't any hurry.

Banjo was a rodeo champion, who used to make money by bulldogging wild pigs – that is, galloping after them on his horse, jumping off his horse and on to a pig, and dispatching it quickly with his bowie knife. Opal prospecting was perhaps less exciting, but certainly more profitable.

'You've got a good show here all right,' said my father, indicating the acres of churned-up dust.

'Yeeaup.'

Banjo did not talk a great deal, but he was positively garrulous compared to the next fossicker we met. I don't remember his name, possibly because he never spoke it. He had not seen a woman for years, not since the time Banjo convinced him that he should go to hospital and have something done about the suppurating sun cancers and sores which covered his body and into which his clothing seemed to have grown. The nurses had attempted to bath him, which so appalled this hydrophobic man that he took off in his pyjamas and was never seen in Winton again. Or so the story goes. When he first saw me he tugged his hat away from the wild black growth beneath it, clasped it to his chest, looked down to where his feet shuffled in the sand and said not a word. A couple of weeks later he had overcome his shyness enough to spend a night

at our camp, though he still could not bring himself to look at me directly. When he rolled out his swag I noticed that he kept food in there – bits of old damper and wads of 'roo meat which he nibbled on before going to sleep.

'In the old days,' my father said, stirring his quart pot of tea with a stick and staring down at a perfect rectangle of black – the entrance to a forty-foot shaft, dug with a hand-pick out of sandstone – 'the fossickers walked out here in pairs. They had a wheelbarrow between them, which they used to cart water in a ten-gallon tin. One would set up camp and dig, while his mate walked forty or so miles to the billabong to fill up the tin. When he'd returned, to take over the digging, the other would set off with the wheelbarrow. Tough customers. You ready to go down now?'

After a story like that it seemed over-pampered to admit fear of the black rectangle. I gulped down my tea, managed a faint 'yes', slung the tools and the bag of candles across my back and descended into the crypt using the rope and mulga stick ladder my father had made. He had already checked that the shaft and the long tunnel which ran at right-angles to it were safe: 'Timbers are good. A few redbacks of course, but they won't hurt you.' Phantom spiders crawled up my trousers and down my collar as I slithered behind him, lizard fashion. It took us ten minutes to reach the face, a little bulbous cave around which ran the seam like a high tide mark. The candles were lit, the torch turned off. We chipped away like meticulous dentists, listening for the clink of metal on silicate, or watching for a flash of candlelight on what would most probably be worthless potch – but might, just might, be gem-quality opal. I felt something shatter under my pick.

Some time during the dinosaur reign a smallish reptile fell into the primordial ooze. A few million years later its skull lay petrified, partially opalised, and embedded under forty feet of stone. Its remains fell to pieces in my hands, leaving only a two-inch-long, needle-sharp, milky opal tooth. Other wonders lay scattered on the surface – chunks of opalised sandstone, which looks as if someone had pricked the dull red rock all over, then turned on a swivelling, multicoloured light inside it. The Australian bush is full of secret miracles like these. There is a gorge in central Australia where the river sand glitters with banks of garnet chips and mica – Sindbad's valley of jewels.

Next on the list of delights came the waterhole – the only permanent water for a radius of fifty miles. I don't know why arid lands are considered empty of life. Where life gets a toehold it exists in obscene abundance. Where there are ants, there are zillions of ants; where there are butterflies, one cannot breathe the air for them. When birds come to drink at a billabong the air reverberates with their chattering and jostling and the boughs of trees bend under their weight. At night there are too many stars. The rockhole was a mere thirty feet across, but almost as deep. The water was still and cold, and so clear you could see the bottom. Little perch, unused to seeing humans, rose to the surface and ate damper from our hands. At dusk, when the surface of the water was a sheet of orange light and the smooth trunks of gums turned iridescent, kangaroos and wallabies came to drink. Later, brumbies snorted into the night breeze and cautiously came down the white sandy bank.

Our tour of the sights culminated in a sacred one – an Aboriginal ceremonial ground set high in the hills like a desecrated and forgotten temple. Across a large expanse of bare red rock lay spherical stones set out in circular patterns. Wild cattle and brumbies had wreaked havoc with the designs and my father set about trying to restore them. I did not know enough about Aboriginal culture then to realise that we were trespassers stumbling around where we shouldn't. Even so, the sadness of the place and its eeriness made us both want to leave.

I do not know how much, if anything, this holiday in western Queensland had to do with my later decision to get myself some camels and traipse around central Australia. Sometimes an idea can sit in the back of your mind like a dozing gorilla in a cage, without your being aware of its presence. What was clear to me at the time was that I was torn between two Australias, as different from each other as they could possibly be. My mind had been fed on the adrenalin running in city gutters, but my spirit belonged in the bush.

Nevertheless I took myself back to Brisbane, found a job and set about studying Japanese in a desultory fashion. I shared, with friends, one of the most beautiful houses in the world, whose wide verandas looked over the leafy suburb of Toowong. There used to be many more of these graceful nineteenth-century houses, lending a kind of colonial tranquillity to an otherwise nondescript city, before the developers took to them with sledgehammers and Bjelke's blessing.

In the steamy heat of December 1972 I sat with a group of friends around a television set, getting high on victory and XXXX beer. For the first time since my conception Labor was in office, with such a strong majority in the lower house that none of us worried too much that it did not have control of the Senate. The new government had inherited inflationary policies, and in the year before its election unemployment had trebled. Australia was, as always, caught up in America's economic difficulties. Even so it was a heady time, and for a while the electorate was delighted by the changes, especially the increase in wages. Whitlam moved at a fantastic pace, introducing 114 bills in the first sitting of Parliament. Voters, used to the slow machinations of the previous lot, were breathless and perhaps just a little bewildered. He established diplomatic relations with China; ended conscription; released conscientious objectors from prison; abolished the remnants of the White Australia policy; set about improving the position of Aborigines and women (though not in Queensland); and increased spending on education and culture.

The new Prime Minister represented everything Joh Bjelke Petersen opposed. Backed by businessmen who feared an assault on the very existence of private enterprise, the Queensland Premier waged a relentless campaign against Labor's

Former Labor Premier Gough Whitlam tends the barbie for a pre-election picture taken in 1974

reformist policies. 'I don't want to be political,' he once told the *National Times*, 'but you can't trust the ALP.' One of Whitlam's greatest mistakes was to underestimate the political strength of an opponent who would be one of the prime movers behind his eventual demise.

Living in Queensland then was to be beset by a feeling of powerlessness. The flowering which was taking place in the rest of the country stopped dead at the border, beyond which nothing had changed. Queensland's natural environment was still being chewed up and spat out by overseas companies. Aborigines were in as powerless a position as ever. Every time Bjelke took on Canberra, he seemed to win.

The house where I lived was an idyllic setting in which to vegetate. Tropical breezes wafted through the custard apple trees and played along the length of veranda where I sat with my friends, drinking quietly but steadily, wondering why we all felt so aimless. I half-read anthropological texts, but skipped over the difficult bits (you need a degree in mathematics to understand Aboriginal kinship systems). Inevitably I would let the book fall and return to the gin and one of those meandering conversations with intimate friends concerning the state of the world and what the temperature might be. Nor was I the only one afflicted with this malaise. More and more acquaintances, disillusioned with politics, were drifting off to the country and the alternative lifestyle, carrying copies of the Whole Earth Catalogue. Those who remained congregated at the Royal Exchange pub, there to compete over who could get the most drunk or be the most cynical. The beer garden was taken over by a tattered little army, demoralised by defeat.

On 11 November 1975, a date which can still light fires in the eyes of some Australians, the Governor-General, Sir John Kerr, a Whitlam appointee, dismissed the government and ordered an immediate general election. Shock waves swept through the country. 'Maintain your rage!' declaimed Whitlam to stunned crowd gathered at Parliament House. The new leader of the opposition, Malcolm Fraser, a Victorian pastoralist, had been accusing the government of economic irresponsibility. The voters were worried. The 'loans affair' soured them further.

The Mining Minister, Rex Connor, had been attempting to borrow four thousand million petrodollars with which to buy back mineral and energy equity from overseas interests. Believing that the Loans Council would thwart the scheme, he attempted to avoid having to get its approval by saying the loan was for 'temporary purposes' only. When the opposition seized on the method of borrowing, the merits or demerits of 'buying back the farm' were lost in the mud-slinging which followed. Rex Connor was dismissed for misleading Parliament, along with the Treasurer, Dr Jim Cairns. Meanwhile, Bjelke had been waiting for his chance.

When a Queensland Labor senator died, against all convention Bjelke hand-picked his own candidate, who, despite his ALP membership, announced that he would vote against the Whitlam government on all occasions. The coalition now had the numbers it needed in the Senate to withhold supply. Late in 1975 Fraser announced that he would do just that. Whitlam announced that he would govern without supply. There were no government funds to pay salaries or pensions. The country seemed out of control. It was then that Sir John Kerr decided, after consultations with a Justice of the High Court, to save the nation by dismissing Whitlam and calling for an election.

Constitutional debate raged for months. Press editorials stated that it was wrong of Kerr to seek an opinion from the High Court, and wrong of the judge to offer one. The dismissal had occurred under section 64 of the Constitution, which states that the 'Minister of State shall hold office during the pleasure of the Governor-General'. But nobody had ever supposed that this should be taken literally; it was a courtesy only. Labor supporters came out to demonstrate, eggs were thrown at Kerr's car; Fraser kept up his attacks on government spending, frightening an already bamboozled electorate. 'If this doesn't bring Australians out on the street,' said an astounded friend when the news came through, 'nothing will.' But the sad truth was that the majority of voters were concerned neither with reform nor with constitutional issues. They were concerned with maintaining an extremely affluent lifestyle which they had come to believe was a birthright. They voted Fraser in with the biggest parliamentary majority since Federation. Fraser did indeed bring down inflation by controlling government spending. The cost to Australia was an explosion of unemployment.

A Labor minister of the Whitlam era once said:

Australia's past shortcomings . . . have sprung in large measure from a vague and generalised fear of our own environment, the feeling of being alien in our own continent and our own region. As a result, we have tended to swing between isolationism and interventionism, between 'Fortress Australia' and an over-dependence on one great powerful protector; and culturally, between slavish imitation and brash self-assertion. What is sometimes called a new nationalism, for which the election of this government is seen as a catalyst, is, I hope, really the beginning of self-confidence. . . . My great hope for my Government, however long it may endure, or as my opponents would say, be endured, is that it will see the end of the old inhibitions, the self-defeating fears about Australia's place in the world, and the beginnings of a creative maturity.

There are many who cannot forgive Whitlam for his mistakes, of which there were many. But Australia did see 'a period of creative maturity' during his term of office. His government improved the quality of life for large sections of society, and in my opinion we didn't have nearly enough of him.

Just before Whitlam's fall the gorilla of an idea which had been dozing peacefully in the back of my mind woke up, started beating its chest and demanding that I get out of Brisbane. Many people have asked me why, but why, did I decide to take myself to the middle of nowhere, work for two years to get myself some camels, then drag them across half a continent full of emptiness and flies. I still don't know the answer. It just seemed at the time like a good and not terribly remarkable idea. Australia may have been feeling the pinch, but it was still an economic paradise compared to the 1980s and I was fairly certain that there would be work available in the Alice. A sense of adventure is so much easier to develop where there is also some sense of financial security. Often the people who ask the question are ignorant (as I was) of how extraordinary and addictive a place Alice Springs is. Nor are they aware that Australia's deserts are anything but empty. This is not surprising. The vast majority of Australians have not been west of the Blue Mountains, and would prefer to take their holidays in Bali than in the backlands. Nor have they ever seen, much less spoken to, Aborigines, who are concentrated in non-urban regions.

The train which runs due north from Adelaide to Alice is called the Ghan, after the immigrant Afghans who built it at the turn of the century with the aid of their camels. In doing so, they put themselves out of business: trains and trucks took the place of camels as desert transport. The 'ghans' let their herds go, and it was from this feral source that I hoped to get a couple of my own.

The first few days following one's arrival in a distant location are invaluable for the clarity of perception they offer, a clarity which wears off as the distant location turns into the place where one lives. There was nothing subtle about the Alice: it hit me like a brick in the head. I had landed on the frontier, where so many of the forces at work in Australian society were in visible conflict. Alice has it all. Ideologues of the right; ideologues of the left; indescribably ugly suburbia growing cancerously out into the scrub; the scrub retaliating with dust-storms and floods. Rural conservatism; southern do good-ism; an American installation at Pine Gap; swarms of the peace demonstrators whom it attracts; awesome landscape; neat back yards with sprinklers, bald lawns and dried out dahlias; business interests welcoming the tourists with plastic bunting and bus trips; old timers bemoaning the garbage left at their secret picnic spots. But the fundamental tension in Alice Springs is between Aboriginal culture and European – the black and white of the place.

When I first went there it was a small, dusty, dismal place with no fruit and vegetable shop. Now it is a large, dusty, dismal place with not only fruit and vegetable shops but patisseries and a casino as well – an embryonic Reno whose rate of growth is staggering. The first antithesis that struck me was of the town to its environment. It sits like a chunk of bessa-brick set in pure gold filigree. Seeing the Macdonnell Ranges at dawn made the back of my neck tingle. So, for different reasons, did my first visit to the pub. The denizens were out to impress a city girl with their knowledge of local customs. I learned that coons had thicker skulls than whites, so that when you hit them with crowbars nothing broke. I learned that all coons were potential rapists of white women and that all female coons ('black velvet') were drunken whores. From some of the bleary-eyed, beer-gutted men I learned that coons couldn't handle booze. I learned that a local politician's wife had suggested that coons be used to pull rickshaws full of tourists from the airport, ten miles outside town. Coons were dirty. Coons were dogs. Coons were giving the place a bad name. I have often been accused of painting a very negative picture of the Alice of those days. But what a young white woman travelling alone will hear and see is quite different from what a person in a more protected situation will hear and see. Alice was displaying her gutters to me with innocent bravado. Since then she has cleaned up her act. Generally speaking, racism in the town has become more urbane and cautious in its expression: blatant racism was bad for tourism.

There is no doubt that life has improved for the majority of Aborigines who live there, but it is an improvement won by their own efforts and organisation and by their alliance with some supportive Europeans who came to the Alice at about the time that Whitlam introduced the Aboriginal Land Rights (Northern Territory) Act. It was finally enacted, with some amendments, by the new Fraser government in 1976. For the first time traditional Aborigines were able to make claims to ancestral lands, but only in the Northern Territory, and only to unoccupied and unalienated Crown land. The legislation did not provide for those people who perhaps needed some form of compensation most – those who had been taken away from their country and forced to live in towns, cities or settlements. Even so, the act marked a turning point in Aboriginal and white relations in Australia. A Commissioner was appointed to hear the claims, and a Central Land Council was set up in the Alice to represent the owners and to advise them how to manage and control the land.

Traditional Aborigines are only nomadic over a fixed and specific area of country to which they belong. The notion of people owning land, rather than land owning people, is, in terms of their own law, nonsense. Land to them is a religious phenomenon. They believe that the earth's topography was formed by their ancestors – spirits who came from the time of creation (the Dreaming), who journeyed across Australia and established sacred sites. Descendants of these Dreamtime heroes must protect the sites through ritual and ceremony. The people belonging to a particular piece of land have a spiritual responsibility for it – indeed an individual's whole identity is bound up with that piece of land. Sacred objects – tchuringas – are something like title deeds to the land of each clan.

This concept of land tenure is complex, to say the least, and diametrically opposed to any European one. Translating it into Australian property law presented enormous difficulties for the anthropologists, linguists and lawyers employed to work on land claims, and for the Aborigines themselves. Much of their sacred law is also secret. Having to divulge such secrets placed both

Opposite above: Pubs in Australia are largely a male preserve. At one in Alice Springs 'I learned that coons had thicker skulls than whites, so that when you hit them with a crowbar nothing broke...'

Opposite below: Cattle hands at an outback rodeo in Queensland drown their thirsts after a hard and dusty day

men and women under enormous stress. I watched, on video, one of the claim hearings. It was held out bush. The judge, lawyers, anthropologists and some Aborigines were sitting at trestle tables; others sat cross-legged on the ground. It was time for one very old woman to sing a ceremonial song, proving her connection to her country. She got up, bowed her head and, weeping and hesitant, began whispering her song, everything about her betraying an intolerable anguish.

Months of preparation went into these claims, as evidence was collected and the information put together in a way that the court could understand. Hitherto hidden complexities in the structure of Aboriginal society, and the revealing of further layers of intellectual refinement in Aboriginal culture, continue to astound anthropologists.

Naturally there was a furious white backlash, and some locals were literally up in arms. Their principal objections were that Aborigines were being given something which whites were not (given the disparity between the living standards of whites and blacks, and the history which gave rise to the disparity, this was the most obscene criticism); that Aborigines would form a separate 'nation'; and that Aboriginal control of land would hinder or prevent mining. On the other side it was hoped that, with land, Aborigines would be able to begin to make their own choices and decisions, to control their own lives and to negotiate with whites on more equal terms. The reality was that they were very far from being on anything like an equal footing. Nor did they have the kinds of resources with which to put forward their views, as did the multinationals who wanted free access to their land, or the government forces which were trying to undo the legislation. In some cases negotiations with mining companies were beneficial to both sides – royalties were one of the few ways in which communities could earn money. But now that the land was under their control they could protect sacred sites and they could keep alcohol out of their settlements.

Aboriginal communities are still in crisis, and there is now a danger that sympathetic whites will wipe their hands of the whole business and declare that enough has been done. When I returned to Alice in 1987 I talked to a friend who works for the Pitjantjatjara health service, which caters for a population of two and a half thousand and covers a vast desert area of traditional lands the size of Wales. Out of that population of two and a half thousand, the health service copes with forty-five thousand cases per year. All the diseases can be attributed to poverty – kidney failure, diabetes, heart disease, trachoma, perforated ear drums and malnutrition. Most of the children are partially deaf and therefore unable to learn. Concern for Aboriginal welfare has become much less fashionable in the 1980s, just at a time when the small gains they have made need consolidation and support, and the problems they still face need a radical rethink. Although the current Labor government, led by Mr Hawke, has promised federal land rights legislation, nothing has been done. Responsibility is shuffled between state and federal bureaucracies. At 1 per cent of the population Aborigines have no ballot power, and they feel betrayed. On one of my visits there I saw some graffiti on a wall surrounding one of the flash clubs: 'Surrender white man your town is surrounded.' Necessary irony for a group of people who, no matter how many gains they make, will always be confronted with a tidal wave of development threatening to engulf them.

At the time of my first visit, in the mid-1970s, so involved were my friends in the land rights struggle, and so preoccupied was I in getting my camels to sit on command, that no one paid much attention to what went on behind the high wire fences which surrounded the white domes of Pine Gap, the American spy base just beyond Alice Springs. They looked like giant puffballs stuck out there in the ranges: beautiful in their way, and poisonous. Since then the opposition to Australia's willingness to have American bases on her soil has become increasingly loud. Pine Gap is the most important American installation outside the USA and it has turned Alice Springs into a nuclear target. Yet the Australian people have never been allowed a say in whether they think the supposed benefits are worth the risks, nor have they been given information on which to make an informed decision. The government has given assurances that Pine Gap aids nuclear deterrence, but it has not discussed its less benign potential. If the USA moves away from the policy of nuclear deterrence towards the doctrine of winnable nuclear war, the Australian bases can be used for aggressive purposes, and it is the US government which will make the decisions on how these bases will be used, not its Australian counterpart. Pine Gap is also essential to Reagan's Star Wars programme. Meanwhile the Australian government shakes a fist at the French government for its bomb tests in the Pacific, while continuing to sell to them the uranium with which to make the bombs. . . .

By April 1977 I had trained my camels to sit on command, and I had trained myself in the ways of the desert. Originally I had intended to wander fairly aimlessly, but because I had involved an American magazine in the journey I now had to give it a structure – Alice Springs to the Indian Ocean, seventeen hundred miles of desert and semi-desert. The trip would take me through Aboriginal settlements and cattle stations, across a few waterless tracts, and into some of the most awesome country in the world. I had been preparing myself for it for two years; the journey itself took nine months. Nine months of blessed solitude, interrupted, towards the end, by the totally unexpected arrival of the press. I have described the camel trip more often than I care to think about, and I don't want to repeat myself here. Let me simply say that as I sat on the beach at journey's end, watching the sun melt into the Indian Ocean, I thought I could take on anything. Four days later I was in New York writing a story for the American magazine.

This was my first trip abroad. I was in a dazed state. Only a few days before I had been certain of who I was. Alas, I was about to understand, just as Aborigines had understood for some time, that the power to describe rests with the powerful. It was in America, and later in England, that I learned what Australia was – an outpost, a colony, *terra incognita*. I discovered that in Australia the moon was upside down, and water went down the plughole the wrong way. I discovered that Europe and America were not a long way from Australia, but that Australia was a long way from anywhere. So far, in fact, that few people knew about it except that it was populated by sun-tanned men who wore corks on their hats, that kangaroos delivered the mail, and that people spoke surprisingly good English. Australians sang 'Waltzing Matilda' all the time and weren't very bright. It came as something of a shock to me. People looked at me suspiciously and announced that I didn't sound like an Australian, presumably because I didn't say, 'Ow ya goin', spawt?'

'But I *am* an Australian,' I would say reasonably. '*Ergo*, this is how Australians sound.'

Since then I have been wandering the globe, returning home for long stretches, only to find the itching in my feet uncomfortable. They say that this instinct for travel is a cultural trait, an atavistic sense that we have all been marooned on a desert island far, far from home. Whatever it is, it presents me with a problem – where do I belong? Do I live in England and holiday in Australia, or do I live in Australia and holiday in England? (Would anyone with a sound mind choose to holiday in England?) My excuse for my defection to London is that my work takes me there. It is much easier to write books when it is raining, when the sun doesn't beckon you outside, when friends don't drop by at all hours of the day and night to say things like 'Oh, come on, let's go to the beach/Doyle's seafood restaurant/party/film/play/Kinsella's supper club/out bush/for a picnic/down the coast/sailing – you can always work tomorrow.' In London people tend to leave you alone to get on with it, because they are getting on with it themselves. They ring you up in advance before dropping in. In London, work tends to take precedence over having a good time. Down under, it's not only the moon that's upside down.

In early 1987 I came back after being away for two years, feeling that I had missed out on whatever the events were that had given Australia its present shape. Coming home again was like wading into warm vegetable soup. As if the molecules themselves were having too pleasant and easy a time of it to bother with all that nervous jumping around. I got used to it soon enough, as my own molecules got the hang of it and a slow, vacant smile began to take the place of the perennial cold-country pout. 'What's your hurry, mate?' asked the man who stamped my passport.

It is always through the sense of smell that I first recognise a place – recognise its claim on me. The minute I stepped out into the night a tangle of smells – dry grass, fresh, clean dust, ocean – captured me like tendrils, anchored me down, and I knew that I was home. I could see the familiar shape of banksias silhouetted against the sky. The moon was bulging and golden, only distantly related to that icy, pale, diminished, inverted creature of the northern hemisphere. And there was Orion, diving down, as he should, towards the horizon, not leaping up out of it. And with the sensual recognition of home came a soothing of some inner disturbance that I had not been aware of.

I do not know what it means to love a country, and I lack the patriotic belief, so prevalent in Australia at the moment, that the place of one's birth is above criticism. But I know what Joseph Conrad meant when he said in *Lord Jim* that we return home 'to meet the spirit that dwells in the land – a mute friend, judge and inspirer'.

The taxi driver was an Asian-Australian, friendly and willing to talk. Naturally, my first question was, 'How's everyone coping with the economic downturn?' I was expecting, I suppose, a London-style horror story of belligerence and decline.

'Ah, she'r be light,' he said cheerily. 'Onry fault of unions.'

Dutifully I put forward another point of view, but he shrugged and smiled as if to indicate that economic downturns happened a long way off both in time and space, and besides it was too pleasant an evening for debate. He turned the conversation, instead, to more important matters – his domestic difficulties. We commiserated all the way from Perth to Fremantle – twenty miles. He said, 'How came you rive over there? Austraria the best counly in the world.'

I could not think of a suitable reply. I was being undone by the warmth of that velvety breeze. And the smell, oh God, that smell. I was sure there was a hint of mango in it. We passed a road sign saying, 'G'day, welcome to W.A.'

It was three in the morning when I arrived at the house where I would be staying. I had never met my hosts – they were friends of friends – but they welcomed me without fuss or formality, with a warm familiarity that is unique to Australia. I had been missing that too, I discovered; the kettle was on, the bed made up. They lived in an old church hall: there were paintings all over the walls and yellow moonlight drained in through arched windows. A fan beat lethargically from the high ceiling next to jungly, dangling plants. I sent them off to bed and sat outside under the grapevines and jasmine, waiting for the dawn, listening to ocean noises, wondering why the hell I ever went away.

Even after three or four weeks the feeling of being in a distant location had not worn off. I was still intensely receptive to new impressions, and the strongest impression was that my Australian paradise was a false one. It was quite by chance that I landed in Western Australia just in time to avoid the America's Cup. The pretty coastal port of Fremantle, an old town of bright, bright blue skies, yellow stone buildings and colonial balconies, was unrecognisable. Faded houses had all been painted up, like old biddies with too much make-up on. The Aga Khan had bought a restaurant and was charging the kinds of prices which would guarantee him a millionaire clientele. Down at the quays, tacky hot-dog joints housed blank-eyed women longing for a customer to break the tedium. Commercial interests had gone berserk, hoping to cash in on what everyone assumed would be a vast and permanent influx of American tourists.

The America's Cup brought razzmatazz and an air of commercialism to the pretty town of Fremantle in Western Australia. The crew of Kookaburra II

Paul Hogan as Crocodile Dundee, 'the pure myth made manifest'

But the tourists didn't come in the quantities expected, and no one, it seems, had seriously considered that we would lose the Cup. Well, Dennis Connor has taken it back, the tourists have gone home, businessmen are bemoaning their loss of capital and shortly Fremantle will look like a gaudy little ghost-town, recovering slowly from its brush with progress. How long it will take the national psyche to recover from the loss of the Cup is another question.

What has happened in Fremantle is a microcosm of what has happened to the rest of the country. Everywhere there is a brash, commercial nationalism. To breathe any form of criticism of Australia is to be thought captious or depressing or un-Australian. People who a decade ago might have said, 'If it's from overseas, it's good,' are now tending to say, 'If it's Australian it's the best and I'll biff any bastard who says different.' Billboards advertise Colonial this and Aussie that, Down-Under mufflers and Koala duvets. Television jingles assure us that we are proud to be Australian. But it's an insane nationalism, because unless some drastic changes are made Australians will have nothing left to feel nationalistic about.

Inflation has hit 10 per cent and our unemployment statistics rival those of Britain. But just as Australians did not consider what would happen if they lost the America's Cup, so they refuse to listen to the gurgling sound Australia is making as it goes down the economic plughole the wrong way. It is a country without focus, led by a man who seems not to know what he believes in any more. Except for a tiny minority, no one is thinking in the long term; most people continue to believe that we can borrow our way out of anything. Australia is now the third largest debtor nation in the world. Soon the whole country will be owned by huge European, Japanese and – especially – American companies.

The great grey area of Australia's middle class cannot think, it seems, past the quarter-acre plot, the two cars and the hefty mortgage. They take the good life for granted rather than as something which has to be struggled for. They refuse to accept that the downturn will very shortly begin to affect them, and are unprepared for the fact that soon not only will there not be enough prawns for the barbie, but there will be no barbie on which to cook them. When the bubble bursts, will Australians be forced to *think*? Or will we continue to search for easy answers, as we have in the past?

Such questions filled my thoughts as I sat down to watch television one day in early 1987. There was old Sir Joh Bjelke Petersen uttering the usual formula phrases at the interviewer – something about 'lighting a bush fire in Australia', something about how you 'can't walk with a foot on either side of a barbed wire fence', something about how the people who disagreed with him should 'jump in the lake' – the stuff which always raises a smile on the faces of suave southerners. And there was one of his National Party supporters in Wagga Wagga giving the usual spiel about stopping 'tax money going to homosexuals, lesbians, Aboriginals and all this trash'. Just a few days before I'd been reading of Joh's support of Bruce Ruxton, the head of the Returned Soldiers' League, who had recently lashed out at Archbishop Desmond Tutu, calling him 'a black thug, the bottom of the barrel'. And I had just read of the race riots in Goondiwindi, Queensland. 'Nothing changes,' I thought.

Then I felt a quick chill run down my spine. Bjelke had also said something about becoming Prime Minister. I turned up the volume and listened, appalled, as he fulminated against the unions and promised the electorate a flat rate 25 per cent income tax when he became PM. The political pundits smiled at his ravings, as they always have. Hawke was smirking when he announced that Bjelke was destroying the opposition by threatening to set up a new 'Joh' party. Was I the only one worrying? Was I the only one remembering how Joh had won so many battles in the past? Was I the only one taking seriously the fact that Australia was ripe for just the kinds of easy answers that someone like Bjelke Peterson offers?

Later, I watched as some coalminers were asked what they thought of him. These men probably earn something like $50,000 a year. They are in a high tax bracket.

'If he's going to give us a twenty-five per cent tax cut, you bet we'll vote for him,' they said.

'But surely,' said the interviewer, 'you are traditional Labor supporters?'

This did not worry the miners, concerned as they were with more prawns for the barbie. What they did not see was that if Joh, or someone like him, did get in, they would shortly find themselves earning $20,000 a year, and their union would be powerless.

Is Australia trying to self-destruct? After all, our favourite song, 'Waltzing Matilda', is about a cheerful suicide. And if I stayed here, would it stop bothering me? Would I join the crowds strolling down the beach, lost in an agreeable somnolence, confident that disaster could never happen here, while a tiny minority hang their heads in frustration and shame? I feel a painful ambivalence to the Lucky Country – an ambivalence which makes it difficult to live here but even more difficult to live anywhere else.

Before I left London, my niece took me to see the film *Crocodile Dundee*. I hadn't wanted to go, but within two minutes I was hooked. I laughed in spite of myself. I laughed because of myself. There, on the big screen, was the pure myth made manifest. There was Australia as it would like to be seen, as it would like to see itself. Innocent, utterly lacking in pretension, gallant, self-parodying, quietly confident, open-hearted, masculine, laconic, egalitarian, easy to patronise, but able to take the piss out of smart Alecs, and under all that toughness and bravado the heart of a pussy cat and a spirit full of wilderness. It was as if Australia, the most urbanised and now the most multi-cultural society in the world, had, in its search for an identity, copied what the rest of the world thought of it. The sentimental caricature has always been far from the truth, but never more so than now.

Picture
Acknowledgements

PHOTOGRAPHS: Contents Pages: Tom Keneally photographed by Douglass Baglin, Patsy Adam-Smith by Richard Taylor and Robyn Davidson by Peter Drewe. Frontispiece: Royal Australian Historical Society. Pages 12, 16 (top) Axel Poignant Archive; 16 (bottom) Mitchell Library, State Library of New South Wales; 21 (top) Axel Poignant Archive; 21 (bottom) BBC Hulton Picture Library; 24 Popperfoto; 24–25 Melbourne Public Library; 28 (both) BBC Hulton Picture Library; 30 (top) J. Allan Cash; 30 (bottom) BBC Hulton Picture Library; 33 (top) Banana UK, Southampton; 33 (bottom), 34–35 Colorific!/Rick Smolan; 34 (inset) Stephen Benson Slide Bureau; 38 (top) Axel Poignant Archive; 38–39 Robert Harding Picture Library; 39 (top) Weldon Trannies/Leo Meier; 40 Ardea/Jean-Paul Ferrero; 44 Bruce Coleman/David Goulston; 44–45 Mitchell Library, State Library of New South Wales; 47 Museum of Applied Arts & Sciences, Sydney; 48–49 Mitchell Library, State Library of New South Wales; 52 Popperfoto; 53 (top) La Trobe Collection, State Library of Victoria; 53 (bottom) Mortlock Library, State Library of South Australia; 55 (top) Patsy Adam-Smith/State Library of Victoria; 55 (bottom) Popperfoto; 57 (top) BBC Hulton Picture Library; 57 (bottom) Archives Office of New South Wales; 58 Popperfoto; 58–59 Camera Press/Harold Pollock; 60–61 Axel Poignant Archive; 66 (top), 67 from *Ned Kelly: The Authentic Illustrated Story* compiled and written by Keith McMenomy, published by Curry O'Neil Ross Pty Ltd, 1984; 66 (bottom) La Trobe Collection, State Library of Victoria; 68 (left), 69 (right) Mitchell Library, State Library of New South Wales; 71 (both) Popperfoto; 73 Weldon Trannies/Reg Morrisson; 74–75 Aspect Picture Library/John Garrett; 75 (top) Weldon Trannies/Leo Meier; 75 (bottom) Colorific!/Hary Chapman; 76–77 Weldon Trannies/George Hall; 78–79 John Peel; 79 (inset) Axel Poignant Archive; 80 (bottom) Bruce Coleman/John R. Brownlie; 83 (top) Mitchell Library, State Library of New South Wales; 83 (bottom) Museum of Applied Arts & Sciences, Sydney; 84 (top) Mitchell Library, State Library of New South Wales; 84 (bottom) Battye Library, State Library of Western Australia; 86 (top left) Patsy Adam-Smith; 86 (bottom left) Mansell Collection; 86–87 Museum of Applied Arts & Sciences, Sydney; 90 Popperfoto; 91, 93 Archives Office of New

PICTURE
ACKNOWLEDGE-
MENTS

South Wales; 97 (top) Telecommunications Museum, Adelaide; 97 (bottom) Patsy Adam-Smith/State Library of Victoria; 100, 100–101, 104, 105 (both), 107 Australian War Memorial; 110 (top) Patsy Adam-Smith; 110 (bottom) Museum of Applied Arts & Sciences, Sydney; 113 Aspect Picture Library/J. Alex Langley; 114–115, 115 (top) Colorific!/Penny Tweedie; 115 (bottom) Axel Poignant Archive; 116–117 Stephen Benson Slide Bureau; 117 (inset) Colorific!/Penny Tweedie; 120 (top) Bruce Coleman/Jon Allen; 120 (bottom) Stephen Benson Slide Bureau; 122 (both) Mansell Collection; 123 Photo Source/Fox Photos; 124 (top) Museum of Applied Arts & Sciences, Sydney; 124 (bottom) Keast Burke Collection, National Library of Australia; 126, 127 Patsy Adam-Smith; 130 (top) New South Wales Government Printing Office; 130 (bottom) Popperfoto; 131 Mansell Collection; 134 (top) Photo Source/Fox Photos; 134 (bottom) Photo Source/Central Press; 136, 136–137 BBC Hulton Picture Library; 139 (top) Popperfoto; 139 (bottom) Axel Poignant Archive; 141 (top) Popperfoto; 141 (bottom) Patsy Adam-Smith; 144–145 BBC Hulton Picture Library; 145 Photo Source/Keystone; 150 (top) Popperfoto; 150 (bottom) Patsy Adam-Smith; 153 Chris Fairclough Colour Library; 154 John Peel; 155 (top) Colorific!/Penny Tweedie; 155 (bottom) Bruce Coleman/Jan Taylor; 156–157 Bruce Coleman/Eric Crichton; 158–159 Chris Webb; 159 (inset) Colorific!/Frank Herrmann; 160 Camera Press/Fred Coombs; 163 (both), 167 (top) Patsy Adam-Smith; 167 (bottom) Popperfoto; 171 (top) Weldon Trannies/Ray Joyce; 171 (bottom) Colorific!/Cary Wolinsky; 174–175, 175 Photo Source; 178 (both) Photo Source/Keystone; 180 Camera Press; 181 (top) Popperfoto; 181 (bottom) Photo Source/Fox Photos; 183 Camera Press/George Lipman; 186 (top) Camera Press/David Moore; 186 (bottom) Aspect Picture Library/Tom Nebbia; 190–191 Camera Press; 191 Axel Poignant Archive; 193 Colorific!/Rick Smolan; 194–195 Colorific!/D. & J. Heaton; 196 Colorific!/Rick Smolan; 197 Planet Earth/Transglobe/Gunter Deichmann; 198 (both), 199 Colorific!/Rick Smolan; 200 Weldon Trannies/Reg Morrisson; 206 Photo Source/Central Press; 210–211 Popperfoto; 211 Photo Source/Keystone; 214 Weldon Trannies/© John Fairfax and Sons; 215 (top) Aspect Picture Library; 215 (bottom) Camera Press/Jo Giordano; 220 Camera Press/Jennifer Humphreys; 223 Popperfoto; 226 BBC Hulton Picture Library; 231 (top) Weldon Trannies/Colin Beard; 231 (bottom) Camera Press/Basil Williams; 236–237 Weldon Trannies/Brendon Read; 238 Kobal Collection; 241 Axel Poignant Archive.

PAINTINGS: Pages 20–21 *Natives of New South Wales as seen in the Streets of Sydney*, hand-coloured lithograph by Augustus Earle, from *Views in New South Wales*. Rex Nan Kivell Collection, National Library of Australia; 36 (top) *The Conciliation*, 1840, by Benjamin Duterrau, oil on canvas, 121.2 × 170.5 cm. Collection Tasmanian Museum & Art Gallery (purchased 1945); 36 (bottom) *Australian Gold Diggings* by E. Stocqueler. National Library of Australia; 37 (top) *Hyde Park, Old Days of Cricket* by T. H. Lewis. Dixson Galleries, State Library of New South Wales; 37 (bottom) *Eureka Stockade* by B. Ireland. La Trobe Collection, State Library of Victoria; 68 *Burke and Wills at Mount Hopeless*, watercolour by George Lambert. Bendigo Art Gallery; 80 (top) *The Trial*, 1947, by Sidney Nolan. Australian National Gallery; 118 'Lost', 1886, by Frederick McCubbin (1855–1919, Australian), oil on canvas, 115.8 × 73.7 cm. Felton Bequest, 1940, National Gallery of Victoria; 119 (top) *Shearing the Rams*, 1890, by Tom Roberts (1856–1931, Australian), oil on canvas (lined onto board), 121.9 × 182.6 cm. Felton Bequest, 1932, National Gallery of Victoria; 119 (bottom left) *A Call from the Dardanelles*, 1914–1918, by H. M. Burton, poster, 100 × 74 cm. Australian War Memorial (V5167); 119 (bottom right) *One Sunday Afternoon in Townsville*, 1942, pencil & crayon with watercolours, 33.2 × 45.6 cm. (sight). Australian War Memorial (21350).

Index